THE PUPIL

THE PUPIL

A Memory of Love

Monk Gibbon

WOLFHOUND PRESS

© 1981 Monk Gibbon

Published by Wolfhound Press
68 Mountjoy Square, Dublin 1

British Library Cataloguing in Publication Data

Gibbon, Monk
  The Pupil.
   1. Gibbon Monk – Biography
   2. Poets, Irish – 20th century – Biography
  I. Title
  821'.912   PR6013.123

  ISBN 0 – 905473 – 68 – X

Reproduced from copy supplied
printed and bound in Great Britain
by Billing and Sons Limited
Guildford, London, Oxford, Worcester

To
the memory
of
Elizabeth Hickson

It seems as if words were man's only destiny, and that
he has been created to bear thoughts as the tree to bear
fruit. Man is in a torment until he has produced without, what works, within. His written word is like a
mirror in which he needs to see himself and thus to
assure himself that he exists. Until he has seen himself
in his works he does not feel completely living.

Lamartine.

. . . a book is the product of a different *self* from the self
we manifest in our habits, in our social life. . . . If we
would try to understand that particular self, it is by
searching our own bosoms, and trying to reconstruct it
there. Nothing can exempt us from this pilgrimage of
the heart.

Proust.

PREFACE

Anatole France maintained that love was a distressing complaint, invented by the poets. They infected others who, but for them, would never have caught the infection. I should not like to think I was a carrier. Let no impressionable young man in the teaching profession imagine, as a result of reading my narrative, that he has lost his heart to one of his charges.

What I have to tell is not invention. All I am aiming at is to make an acknowledgement of past happiness. I have never forgotten my delight as a schoolboy when I first encountered Virgil's memorable phrase, 'Haec olim meminisse juvabit' – 'It will be a source of pleasure to us one day to have remembered these things.' Feeling instinctively that this was true, I made it the title of one of my prentice poems.

Now after a long interval and with the aid of my journal I am retracing my steps and bridging the years. Geographically, I have had a series of lives. My twelve years in Dorset formed one of these. Though I find places important, it is doubtful if location has ever been the determining factor in deciding what for me was to be memorable: rather it has always been the degree of feeling educed by events and people which has given a place its importance. The whole process of recollection is selective. Memory, like the dual-visaged god Janus, can face two ways. Those who elect to dwell upon sadder days need to be constitutionally pessimistic. The majority of us favour happiness, not merely contentment but those occasions when we experienced a radiant acceptance of heightened awareness.

Each of us decides for himself what is or is not of importance to him. What are we here for? To eat, to drink, to sleep, to make love, to copulate, to raise a family, to die? There is always the further obligation upon us, not merely to live but to feel life deeply. My response to the brief presence of Anne de Selincourt in the school at Swanage proves, if nothing else, that I was capable of feeling. The great majority of people brush aside enquiries which they cannot or do not feel inclined to answer with a dismissive, "Oh, it was nothing really." But I take just the opposite view. I feel inclined to say, "It was everything, or almost everything."

Occasionally, I chance upon a record of emotional experience particularly acceptable to me. To adapt what Charles II said of certain people who had been singing the praises of a rather stupid bishop to him, "I suppose his nonsense suits their nonsense," in like manner I suppose that I approve those writers whose sentiments are most in accord with my own. In Richard Strauss's song *Morgen*, I unquestionably encounter myself. Its words were written by a Scotsman, Mackay, who had been brought up in Germany. In the English prose translation used in the programmes of concert performances, the words by their simplicity and under-emphasis stress the pulsating mood of the occasion.

And tomorrow the sun will be shining again
and on the path that I shall take
it will unite us once more in happiness,
in the midst of this sun-breathing earth . . .
and to the shore, broad and blue-waved,
we shall climb down, quietly and slowly,
wordlessly we shall look into each other's eyes
and upon us will descend the perfect silence of joy.

If I wanted an example of how to convey emotion to others, I would choose what the poet, and equally successfully the composer, have managed to do for us here. I seem to know both place and participants, and can almost feel the warmth of the sunlight as it falls on the sandy track which leads down between high banks towards the dunes and the white line of tiny waves beyond.

Since Mackay's words were written, we have passed into an age when only 'the primal urge' is acceptable as a valid explanation of even the most sublimated personal attachment. It would be philosophic cheating to minimise the importance of that urge in people's lives. It can play an appreciable role even in tentative romance. Sexual tenderness offers itself as a temporary alleviation of love's infinite longing. It is the ultimate expression of mutual approval. But it can also be a frenzied attempt to insist that body must in some way furnish a solution to the predicament into which spirit has led us. In certain individuals it can adopt recognisably absurd disguises, or can manifest itself in ways horrifyingly alien to love. It is not love. So why allow it to take over a word to which it has only partial claim?

In all my twelve years at Oldfeld, I only encountered one pupil – certainly not the one depicted here – who might be said to have voiced her sex as through a megaphone. She was a sixteen-year-old who came to us shortly before the war. And I am inclined to say she was quite unconscious of the effect she produced. There was only a very small modicum of the coquette in her. It was simply that she exuded an aura of sex at every instant. She was a kind of nubile broadcast to remind you that sex existed. I taught her in the top class. She was not actually stupid, but she was certainly not a highbrow. One was tempted to think, as one sat by her correcting an exercise, "My child, you have yet to discover your true significance." No doubt she has since discovered it.

Anne was in an entirely different category. Perhaps the best comparison is with a violin. She was a Stradivarius. She possessed a secret to which even today I cannot be said to have found the key. Was it simply personality, the ability to be openly and unashamedly herself? If she was aware of her effect upon me, it was only in the remote way in which even young children can notice that they have created a favourable impression. I wanted nothing from her. I doubt if I ever consciously felt the need of her regard other than in the mildest degree. All I wanted was her acceptance of what I believed to be my almost imperceptible admiration.

This is not a portrait of the pupil. Rather it is an account of the impact which she had upon me. In a novel she would have to be amplified, exaggerated, reinforced with characteristics from a dozen different sources. And then people would say how true to life it was. But I am not writing a novel and I much prefer to leave her the creature of mystery which she was than to invent fables about her.

It will be an advantage to a reader in this age if he can approach this slender story – direct from life – with an approximation to the mood of the epoch of which it tells. It belongs to 'the thirties'. Viewed in the perspective of 'the eighties', it may seem strange and unreal. But I noted the sequence of events and emotions in considerable detail at the time and I am not inclined to interfere with the substance of that record now. Let it stand. To tell it with anything less than extreme candour would be to rob it of all integrity.

THE PUPIL

I went to Swanage to the big red school on the hill soon after my marriage. In fact our married life, deepening in peace and only now and then ruffled by misunderstanding, can be said to have begun there. We lived at first in rooms in a small private hotel near the school. In autumn and winter the hotel became more like a quiet, well-run boarding-house, sheltering about ten permanent residents who were wise enough to know when they were really well off. I had the best of both worlds, the privacy of an inviolable retreat upstairs, and the amusement of wondering what there would be for dinner. The place was run by an elderly grey-haired lady of great force of character, served by a most excellent staff including her paragon, waiter and general factotum whose name was Louis. It was our great ambition to make the handsome and efficient Louis smile. But he was too professional to allow himself any such indulgence. In all the months that we were there, we only succeeded once. He was the soul of courtesy, but smiling was not listed among his many obligations. I remember, when I had flu as guest of the Chief Justice in Cyprus, there was a Turkish man-servant who had the same inhibition. But he, once he had managed to break his rule, became quite genial. Louis never repeated his single lapse.

From the hotel, we moved to a bungalow which we rented from a friend for a year. I was now even closer to my work. The school was a large, compact, modern and far from unsightly building, on a small hill just outside the town. Adjoining the main building was a tall metal structure topped by a huge revolving wheel. This imposing tower could have been mistaken for a windmill, used to draw artesian water; but it was actually a generator. Connected to a bank of large storage batteries in a nearby shed, it provided electricity for the whole school.

The school building and the wheel stand out in my memory like landmarks. And so do the twelve years I spent there, which were storage batteries of happiness. No doubt I grumbled from time to time, for grumbling is the occupational disease of the schoolmaster; but it never got a real hold on me, and, when I now hear the word Swanage there is a quiet glow of retrospective contentment in my heart.

I remember vividly some of the pupils I taught. In winter, if the playing fields were too wet, I used to take an afternoon 'crocodile' with the boys. We might go down to the public tennis-courts and set out along the sea-front. A small boy named George would attach himself to my side, taking care to occupy this strategic position before the walk had even started. His opening gambit was always the same, "Would you like a story, sir?" "Very much indeed, George." Off he would launch on a melodramatic narrative about Chinamen, detectives, dynamited safes and all the other paraphernalia of penny-dreadful violence. It would flow over my mind like water over a weir. I was thinking of other things. If he said something which seemed to demand comment, I would exclaim, "The devils!" This was like opening a sluice gate, and the narrative would swell afresh in its apparently interminable flow. Generally we would make our way to Peveril Point and, turning back from there, I might allow them to scramble up a steep cleft in the slipper clay from the rocks below. "An absolutely super walk, sir!" would be their verdict. Matron invariably gave me hell when we returned for having allowed their rain-coats to become plastered with grey clay. George never had time to complete his narrative. "I'll have to finish another day, sir," and he would add his usual confession that certain parts of his plot had not been entirely original. "That's all right, George. It was most exciting." No doubt it was, though I hadn't listened to a word of it. I had escaped to a world of my own thoughts, where there were no Chinamen and no dynamite.

The real world was more pressing. At the beginning of the 'thirties Hitler had begun making his 'last territorial claims'. Already we had several German-Jewish children in the school whose parents had decided to get out before the going got even

worse. I had been at Oldfeld for four or five years when one day
the heroic foundress of the school, known to her irreverent staff
and probably to most of her pupils as 'the Old Lady', took me for a
walk on the New Land, bought recently to augment the farm, in
order to consult me on a point of policy. Some parents had
approached her wanting to know if she would take their daughter, a girl of fourteen, in the middle of term. The girl was already
at a famous co-educational school, but was not happy there.

"Any reason?"

"Oh, it has been a ghastly failure, the mother tells me. She was
miserable from the start."

"Why?"

" 'A little of everything' as one of Tolstoy's disciples said to the
Countess when she asked the reason for his marriage having
broken up – in this case, bullying, embarrassing questions about
the facts of life, everything a sensitive nature could be counted
upon to loathe."

"Why don't they send her to a girls' school?"

"She's mad about horses."

"Every fourteen-year-old girl is mad about horses."

One of my reasons for coming to the school had been that part
of my duties would be to teach riding. The memory of two army
riding schools had made me a sympathetic riding instructor.
Many of my pupils took only a few lessons. To get them started as
soon as possible I had worked out a system of "Up, Down! Up,
Down!", urging them to hinge forward at the waist and stand for a
moment in the stirrups while the pony moved at a slow walk.
Then, after twenty minutes of this exercise, their mount was
encouraged into a gentle trot. My monitory Up, Downs! continued, and they soon picked up the rhythm of the new pace.
Most of them got it right by the end of the first lesson. Riding
schools are in no hurry to teach you to rise in your stirrups. They
prefer to let you jolt yourself silly first. But I wanted to press on.
With nervous pupils I never gibed, whatever the stage they happened to have reached. If they were on a horse for the first time
and looked anxious, I'd say, "If you can't hold him at a canter,
we'll just trot. If you're still worried when trotting, then we'll walk.
But don't worry. There's some pace at which you'll feel in control
of the situation, and we'll stick to that pace until you want something more exciting."

It was rewarding to watch a beginner steadily gain confidence, but one needed more accomplished riders to enjoy the wide green expanses of Ballard Down and Nine Barrow Down, or to venture on dune-skirted Studland beach, with the horses pulling on the bit and not a person in sight on the three miles of golden sand ahead. For that reason, it interested me to think that I might be getting another expert.

"What about her work?"

"She has brains, I'm told," and the Old Lady mentioned a name well-known in the literary world. "She's a great niece of Basil de Selincourt who reviewed one of your books so favourably. And both her father and mother are very cultured people."

"Well, I wouldn't mind another good rider. But generally speaking, it's a mistake to snatch a child away from a school and send them elsewhere."

She agreed that this was so.

"If she comes to us now in the middle of the Easter term, she'll be the speckled bird. I don't say the others will harass her, but it's the wrong kind of start."

"That's what I feel myself."

"Let her come in the summer. It's always a good term. And by then, we'll have a better show of horses. Arthur tells me he's going to buy those two ponies from the proprietor of The Ship Inn. His daughter can't manage the larger one."

Arthur was her son in charge of the boys' side; a fair-haired, Nordic-looking individual with a Cambridge M.A. I liked working with him. He was a progressive, with a certain number of indispensable, conservative leanings. His wife Vera was a delightful person, an ex-pupil of the school and widow of a man who had once taught science there. They had two children and three more would presently join the little community up under the roof in the long attic flat at the very top of the building. It was one of the Old Lady's favourite slogans that "A school should be a large family – a small nation." Arthur and Vera provided us with a prototype for the family. They were a touchingly devoted couple; he always busy, she equally busy, yet never in the slightest degree hurried. In later years, like the section of a bee-hive revealed when one side of the hive has been removed and replaced by a pane of glass, I would see this family of seven going about their daily business in the same way that bees go about theirs. School life busied itself about them. It must have been distressing to be forced to live so much in public. They could not escape even when they retired to their attic retreat in the evening. Someone, child or member of staff, was certain to knock at the door with a message or an enquiry. They would find Arthur correcting books at the table, Vera trying a change of diet for the newts in the aquarium on the high window-ledge, and the lady-nurse getting ready to bath the latest baby.

Arthur concurred with my opinion, and the summer term was suggested as the more suitable. Evidently the parents, too, agreed with the Old Lady's views. The girl's name was down on the new school-list when we returned in May. But even then she did not materialise. Rumour said that she was ill. Already something like a legend seemed to have formed about her amongst the other children. They maintained that she was a marvellous horse-woman, almost in the circus-rider class. But it was three weeks before she appeared; and then it transpired that she was not after all going to ride, perhaps on the grounds of expense.

For a time I did not teach her. But in an establishment of only ninety pupils, one soon knows everybody. She was a tall, fourteen-year-old, who looked at least a year older than her age. Her brown bobbed hair was divided down the centre and held back from her round forehead by a narrow band of black velvet. Her features were a little pale and she had large expressive eyes which seemed to be capable of infinite melancholy. Her voice was gay enough on most occasions, though it held slightly ironic inflexions; one noticed a rather clipped, biting incision of speech when she read aloud, as though she were at enmity with the words, or at least wanted to keep them firmly in their place. This mannerism the class immediately learned from her, but as no comment was passed it soon died a natural death. By this time I was taking her for Latin, a subject in which she showed average ability. She was in a form that I taught only once in the course of the day, and then for less than an hour.

You ask if I noticed her? Yes, of course I noticed her. I notice every pupil I teach. Or at least I did in those days. She had had such a build-up; the consultation as to whether she should come or not; her arrival after term had begun; the prospect of having a particularly good riding pupil (though in that I was to be disap-pointed). All this made her a little exceptional, and though she went to no extravagant lengths to assert herself, her individuality soon made itself felt. She was in the fourth form, the last form to have boys and girls in roughly equal number. Our boys went on to their public school at fourteen. In Form IV Anne could indulge in continuous ragging with little Ivor Thomas, a brilliantly clever twelve-year-old. Witty, mischievous and companionable he was sufficiently her junior for her to feel safe with him. And though she got the best of their exchanges he was quite able to hold his own. Their quarrels obviously concealed mutual affection. In fact, they carried them to such lengths that they became known as 'the loving haters'.

At this stage I only taught her Latin. Of her capabilities in English I knew nothing, except that she came from a literary family. She had been with us about a year when I began to hear about her from my colleague Underwood.

Underwood was an illustration of the Old Lady's eclectic taste when it came to choosing her staff. He was a Catholic – with the capital – whereas she herself was a Quaker, and her school had been patronised by the well-known Quaker family the Cadburys, who had shown their gratitude by giving us our large and very well-equipped gymnasium. Of all my colleagues I had most in common with Underwood. He shared my tastes in a number of different directions; in literature; in an enthusiasm for gramophone records, and in a personal preference, which was not concurrent and which, while it lasted, both of us kept very much to ourselves.

Underwood had been at Oxford and was still paying off debts for gramophone records acquired while there. He had fallen under the spell of that strong character and brilliant intelligence, Father Martin D'Arcy, and had become a convert. Once he threw out a brief hint of his motives for this step when he remarked casually to me in conversation, "It was either that or the end of everything for me." With his sleek black hair, good looks, saturnine expression and assumed cynicism, he suggested an intellectual version of the knut of Gilbert Frankau days. But most of the knuts were lying long since in shallow graves under French soil, and the expression was by now almost forgotten.

I owed to Underwood my first glimpse of the newcomer's talent. One of my numerous ex-classroom responsibilities was to be impresario at the school concert on alternate Sunday evenings.

This was a duty which I shared with the music master. Of all our activities, it was perhaps the one most typical of the school. It suggested a cross-section of the Old Lady's methods, mannerisms and ideals. Anyone approving it would approve our general aims and the means we used to achieve them; anyone to whom it seemed strange and a little casual would almost certainly be out of sympathy with the whole of our regime.

For the Sunday evening gathering was at once casual and traditional; formal, and at the same time amazingly flexible. It needed to be, for it addressed itself to an audience varying in age from seven to the mid-seventies. Parents were welcome, and there were nearly always several mothers and sometimes fathers of day-children present. It was held in the dining-hall and even the arrangement of the audience was curious, for some children sat with their backs to the performers. At the end of the dining-room three or four rows of chairs were placed for staff and visitors. All the dining tables remained in their usual place, the great long table under the row of windows which looked out on the terrace, and the other shorter tables at right angles to it. At these sat the children, engaged in sewing, embroidery, knitting, stamp-arrangement, model construction or whatever appealed to them, provided that it could be done silently. Games were not allowed, but any individual activity or craft of a quiet nature was a brilliant solution to what would otherwise have been an insoluble problem. It allowed an eight-year-old to work quietly at a jigsaw while listening to a Beethoven sonata. It let a great writer's words seep into the pores of a thirteen-year-old while he glued together the several parts of a model aeroplane.

We commenced the evening with a rather curious sabbatical gesture. Arthur stood up and gave out the number of a hymn from the top table where he sat with his wife and young children. We rose and sang it. Then we sat down. After an almost imperceptible pause, Arthur gave out another hymn. Whereupon we immediately stood up once more and sang it. We did this four times in rapid succession, resting ourselves on our chairs for a matter of seconds between hymns. Then we put our hymn-books down and the concert began.

I conducted proceedings from half-way down the room, looking across it towards the terrace. My evenings were literary, and more of a problem than the music master's, who could entertain us with class-singing and performances by individual pupils, or even with the aid of an occasional visitor. I had to devise a symposium and play a major part in it myself. But I could count on my wife's help in the matter. She was very closely identified with all school activities. She held an Oxford degree and in time was allowed to stand in for me and take occasional classes while I was riding. She held a blue for lacrosse and a half-blue for net-ball, and before long, was given charge of the senior girls' tennis. They admired her. Years later one of them would tell me how they had regarded her as the acme of feminine poise and good taste. As she had read English at Oxford I welcomed her suggestions for my fortnightly concert. But the responsibility was mine, and often at a quarter-to-six on a Sunday evening I was still in the front hall, seated on a sofa, feverishly turning the pages of anthologies which had already been marked with slips of narrow paper. I had rounded up a dozen intelligent pupils of varied ages, and these were now being 'rehearsed'. I can hear myself saying to one of them:

"No, you must read a bit slower. They won't take it in, if you go at that pace. Give me the book. Now listen. You are Doctor Johnson, a grubby old man who slobbers his food down the front of his clothes. You have been crouching over your table in chill attics for a matter of seven years or more, supporting yourself by hack journalism while you finish your famous dictionary. Now it is nearly complete and the rumour is out that it is going to make you very famous. Seven years ago the illustrious Lord Chesterfield snubbed you and kept you waiting for hours in his anteroom. Since then he has not take the smallest notice of you. Suddenly he has become gracious. He would like to receive the dedication. He wants to appear as your patron. And this is what you write to him; the most terrific snub in history. Don't bother about slobbering down the front of your tunic, but do remember that you have all the bitterness of a tired old man behind your words. . . ."

As title of my literary evening I might choose: "Letters on famous occasions"; or "The lean Spaniard long in prison, a Cervantes programme"; or "Animals in Literature"; or "An evening with the Russians"; and so on. The great thing was to have a theme that united a variety of readings. The school abounded in books. There were crammed bookcases wherever you went. And variety could be achieved by ringing the changes on my readers, as well as by occasionally enlisting a member of the staff. If an excerpt was particularly dear to me, or if I wanted to give it a special, almost personal inflexion, I read it myself. At six o'clock, there was an interval and the younger children gathered up their hobbies and crafts from the green baize-covered tables and went off to bed. We then resumed our programme, having kept back the more highbrow items.

I used to grouse each fortnight as my turn came round, tired of thinking up new material. And yet in a way I enjoyed it. I think it was in the autumn term that Underwood, who had been praising the way in which his flock were tackling *Richard II* (classes had a different play of Shakespeare in their syllabus each term, so that by the end of three years a pupil could have made the acquaintance of as many as nine plays), offered to put on a class reading of one of its scenes the following Sunday. I jumped at this easing of my responsibilities.

"How long will it last?"

"Oh, about twenty minutes."

"Splendid! I'll count on you for twenty minutes. Who have you got to read the part of Richard?"

"Anne. And she's quite good."

It was an understatement. The reading exceeded his guarded forecast for it. Something in the part of the unhappy king seemed to suit the reader; a streak of melancholy, almost of morbidity in her own nature. The pitch of her voice had a curiously flat, plaintive and yet at the same time distinctly musical note. In daily contacts it might hover on the edge of irony, making her seem older than she was, but in the play-reading it was the quintessence of genuine sadness. The school obviously enjoyed the performance. And the Old Lady looked across the room at me as though to say, "I told you we were getting something out of the ordinary." No-one else, even amongst our best readers, could have struck a note of more convincing despair. For the first time, I pitied the self-pitying monarch.

What must the king do now? must he submit?
The king shall do it: must he be depos'd?
The king shall be contented: must he lose
The name of king? o' God's name, let it go:
I'll give my jewels for a set of beads,

My gorgeous palace for a hermitage,
My gay apparel for an almsman's gown,
My figur'd goblets for a dish of wood,
My sceptre for a palmer's walking-staff,
My subjects for a pair of carved saints
And my large kingdom for a little grave,
A little little grave, an obscure grave; ...

I think her parents heard her read on that occasion. They came from time to time on Sunday evenings. It was only a drive of twelve or fifteen miles for them. Her mother in the past had acted with Lillah McCarthy in Shaw's plays, and was a poet and a verse-speaker of distinction. Her father looked young enough to be her brother and was a schoolmaster-cum-author like myself. Neither of them ever sang her praises, but it was plain how much pride and affection went out from these two towards their talented and highly individual daughter. I was to get to know them better as time went on.

Our Sunday concert was followed by an excellent supper for the staff and families in an adjoining room. It was the Raphael classroom by day. I should have perhaps told you that there were no desks anywhere in the school. Classes were small, and one taught from the head of a table covered with green baize cloth to a group of students gathered around it. This took all the 'chalk and talk' out of the proceedings.

The school was a family affair. Oldfeld was no ordinary school. Everything we did was done a little differently. This is not to say that we sought novelty for the sake of novelty, or were the disciples of that crank Neil, who, having written two or three excellent books about his emancipation from the fetters imposed by tradition upon a Scottish dominie in a small rural school, became a celebrity, and founded a school in which the children were said to look bored and unhappy, being allowed to break the windows and paint obscene slogans on the walls whenever they felt the need of being liberated from their repressions.

Our own establishment kept up with new ideas, and was regarded by the other schools in Swanage as distinctly 'advanced'. But actually we were bound by strong ties to the Old Lady's Quaker past. The school for me was a focus point of a whole host of converging and acceptable influences. It had its annoying and chaotic side, which of course led to periodic lamentations from the staff. Nevertheless, it was the nearest thing I have ever experienced to living in a kind of miniature Plato's Republic.

Meals had their problem. The children waited at dinner. Sometimes your plate would arrive held at an angle of forty-five degrees by a seven-year-old whose thoughts were elsewhere. While such duties were doubtless valuable training, they made the meal a protracted one, and the staff had to adjust themselves accordingly. I approved the informality, as well as a weekly-arranged mingling of different ages at the tables, though I drew the line at reading a newspaper between courses like certain of my colleagues, or doing *The Times'* crossword as the Old Lady did; nor do I ever remember seeing my wife – who, before family responsibilities made it impossible, joined us for dinner – succumb to the temptation of knitting, as some people did.

What aroused my irritation most was when we went, so to speak, into committee. I hate the inevitable wastefulness of debate and discussion. There were the Old Lady's confabulations on Sunday evenings after supper when the staff gathered in her small drawing-room off the entrance lounge hall.

This assembly for coffee was ostensibly a social amenity, but we all knew that our hostess regarded it as an opportunity for exchanging ideas, or, worse still, for comment upon the state of the world. Views were expected to be advanced on politics, on the League of Nations, and on other topics of equally vast implication. I hated the occasion, and was almost always the first to rise to my feet and say good-night, though I was often the only one with anything to contribute to many of the topics. There was another confrontation, a fortnightly one, round the supper table on Friday evenings, when every individual pupil was discussed and awarded a 'card' to send home, reporting on his or her Conduct and Diligence. I'll tell you more about that later. What you must realise is the sense of freedom which pervaded our whole community. Nothing ever was done because it was 'the done thing'. Arthur summed up the whole school well when, in some circular to the staff, he wrote: "It must not be forgotten that what we have primarily to teach our children is not how or what to learn, but how to live."

I learned a good deal about living myself. My role of riding instructor – shared with Arthur and his sister Philippa, known through the school as 'Pip' – gave me a roving brief, for riding

lessons were given in ordinary work time. You fished your pupils
out of someone else's class and became correspondingly unpopular for doing so. I was a particularly outrageous offender. If I
knew that a child had saved up for a lesson and if I had no other
class myself, I would prolong that lesson far beyond its normal
length to give value for money. One could take one's cavalcade of
three horses and a couple of ponies on a different route every day
for a fortnight; exploring the lanes, or visiting the great heather-
covered moor which extended to the reed-girt fringes of that vast
expanse of water known as Poole harbour. One could climb a long
sloping chalky track to the downs, and then for a time trot happily
past clumps of gorse. Out on the downs themselves the sweeping
sheep pastures, which take centuries to establish, gave miles and
miles of uninterrupted view. We would canter out, and only when
we turned for home would we give the horses their heads and
allow them to break into a fierce gallop.

Robert Louis Stevenson once confessed in a letter to a friend, "I
was happy once – at Hyères." What an admission. I have been
happy thousands of times in the course of my life. Those days at
Swanage and my morning rides held as much simple happiness as
any man could desire. Most mornings after breakfast I would go
down to the stable on the farm at the back of the school. The
stable was small and dark and had a very distinct atmosphere of
the past, while the farm was reputed to be recorded in Doomsday
Book. One of the farm men, a straw sticking out from one side of
his mouth, would be swilling out the cement floor of the tin-
roofed cowshed on the far side of the yard. He would grin and eye
me with mild and friendly suspicion, for just inside the further
door of the cowshed was a huge iron bin filled with small compact
cubes of cotton cake for the cows, and I had been known to slip
into the shed and fill my pockets with cubes for the horses.
Generally the children were busy with brushes and curry combs
trying to scrape some of the mud off the flanks of the horses,
acquired when they had been turned out to grass and had rolled
madly in the wet field after the ride the day before. With my
arrival, grooming operations would be cut short. Bridles would
be fetched, and I would watch with a certain amusement the
united efforts of three small children to bit a shaggy pony, whose
pendulous underlip presented no problem, but whose clenched
teeth would baffle them. Eventually her mouth would pop open

out of sheer boredom and the bit would be pushed triumphantly in.

We had our reputed ex-racehorse, Lizzie, said to have run at Epsom and, trading perhaps on that fact, highly temperamental. Then there was Wendy, a lady's hunter, with tiny feet, and Cobweb, a wild-eyed pale chestnut, that had injured her back running away with Arthur on Nine Barrow Down and turning a somersault over a five-bar gate. And there were the two black ponies. Later, when these retired, we would make two much-valued acquisitions; the prancing excitable Tinker and his inseparable companion, a grey, Jimmy.

I could spend the rest of the day describing our various rides. Knitson Lane was a favourite, though it entailed a series of gates. One passed periodically through some vast farm paddock, distinguished by that functional untidiness which one forgives a farmer and no-one else: a rusted plough thrown on its side amid nettles; disused timber, roughly piled; an open shed, with a sagging roof, bedded knee-deep in bracken in preparation for the young cattle. Then came another wooden gate, after which the lane resumed its meanderings, between high banks and blackthorn hedges, across a stubble field; every stage of the way different and delightful in its own fashion. A little beyond was another gate where one day a boy, striving while still on horseback to open it for the rest of the ride, flopped off into the deep mud. This gate led up to a second farm house. In summer its uneven, multi-angled roof of Purbeck slabs used to be completely overrun with a vast surge of tiny, white, rambler roses. The house was sheltered by a group of sycamore trees, and a couple of spaniels would dash out from under these, barking loudly, whenever they saw us coming. Further on the lane brought one to a barred iron gate whose sliding bolt was one of the hardest to manipulate. I would find myself protesting: "You'll never do it unless you manoeuvre right up alongside. Push her nose into the hedge. Don't mind a bramble or two. Oh, jump off! It's quickest in the end and we're in a hurry."

On a saddleback between two green hollows where cattle grazed, one came to a third farm, from which a rosy-cheeked old man set out in a low pony cart each morning to drive a huge can of milk to the town. In his great sunny rick-yard brown hens and spangled cocks scratched happily in the fallen straw and hay. A hen taking a dust-bath, or basking in sunshine always offers one of the most contented sights one can encounter. She settles herself in the little trough that she has hollowed out from the earth to fit the shape of her body, wriggles sideways down in it to make herself more comfortable, and, when she has fluffed out all her feathers, lies there in the sun supremely contented, every now and then blinking a sleepy yet beady eye. Occasionally there is a long, slow, meditative chirrup which expresses, as clearly as any sound can, a satisfaction with existence. "Here I am, on the windless side of the rick; the sun is out; my crop is full of carefully gleaned barley grains; the rooster is chasing pullets elsewhere. If you want to know what contentment is, just come here and fluff out your feathers beside me."

I hope I'm not boring you. Maybe you're not interested in country life? I was. I hated to think of myself as a mere pedagogue. I much preferred to be author plus part-time riding instructor. It was a disappointment to me that our newcomer, whose reputation as a rider had preceded her, did not take riding, so that we had no opportunity of judging her prowess. In just the same way, our music teacher had been disappointed. Although she was studying both the violin and the piano, her parents were taking no risks and were dispensing with his services. She continued her lessons with her own teacher when she went home each week-end.

Only after she had been with us a year did I see her ride. Arthur decided to make an addition to the farming instruction which each form regularly received once a week. They were supervised in their agricultural and horticultural pursuits by one of the farm's most trusted hands, the gaitered and courteous Mansfield, who looked like, and probably had been, a groom. To this would now be added enlightenment from me on – to use army language – "the parts of the 'oss". And, if there was time towards the end of the lesson, they might even get a little riding. Anne came with her form. The first time I saw her astride I knew that all we had been told about her aptitude was true. She took the temperamental Lizzie out, bare back, at the end of the class, to turn her loose in the field. She sat her as if she had become part of the animal; her head high, her back straight, her knees gripping the reputed Epsom-runner's shoulders as though in a vice, reins loose, hands low yet in perfect control. A few weeks later she accompanied me at the end of the lesson to the forge on one of the two new purchases, the lively Tinker. She rode 'long', as they say, heels well down, feet not thrust home but with the ball of the foot resting diagonally on the bar of the stirrup. Obviously, she felt completely at home in the saddle. Only the best of my paying pupils were permitted an occasional ride on Tinker. His last owner had been afraid of him. He had run away with both her and her father, and from then on was ridden with a martingale and a heavy barred bit with curb chain. We had no hesitation in putting him on a snaffle. Provided he was allowed always to lead the procession, he was perfectly docile. Take him to the rear and he immediately became a fretful, prancing demon of impatience. I rode him myself, sparing him as much as I could the humiliation of being at the rear, and secretly sympathising with his arrogance. It was just his way of showing spirit.

I apologise for all these digressions. You must regard this as a Conversation Piece, and not just a portrait. I want you to have an idea of the background. I can only suggest my pupil to you by helping you to see her in the appropriate landscape.

I taught her more often now and to me she seemed a talented, precocious, slightly sophisticated young woman, a little too dependent on temperament to achieve good work and with a pseudo-harshness which was really the obverse of sentiment. As I noted quickly, her slightly barbed tongue was often used to protect her more than ordinarily responsive sensibility. When she made a bitter remark, it seemed to be because she suspected that it might be dangerous to feel too much. She was popular with her school-mates, but she made no attempt to noticeably assert herself or to dominate her contemporaries in any way. She was too busy being steadfastly and uniquely herself to have any such fifth-rate aspirations. And yet she was a force in whatever class she found herself, although why it would have been hard to say. She played games well, but never revealed much enthusiasm for them. The school prided itself on its yearly dramatic production, but despite her excellence in elocution, she never made any very marked contribution on these occasions. I believe you could best put it this way. Without being remarkable, she yet managed always to be distinctive. That was her secret.

When I got to know them better, Anne's parents sometimes discussed her with me. "No-one knows the real Anne," her mother said to me one Sunday evening after the concert. And I thought to myself, "How right! No-one knows her. Not even Anne herself."

As time went on I gradually began to discover a little more about her. I saw her frequently as I had a class with her nearly every day. She became explicable to me in the light of her background, a background obviously cultured and sensitive. The whole circumstances of her home life combined to make her take the arts seriously. The moment poetry was mentioned she became a different creature. Whenever we read a poem which she approved, she seemed to vibrate in sympathy with it. It was like seeing a beacon cast a beam of light out over the dark water of the relative indifference of some of her classmates.

I was in a school where it was not regarded as a crime to have views of one's own. We were beginning to hear a lot about 'the century of the Common Man'. I distrusted the phrase. My pupils were not a commonality. They were persons of widely different tastes, energies and abilities on whom it would be fatal to impose a pattern of theoretically laudable but actually down-grading equality. What I had to do was to give everyone a reasonably fair run for his money. I can say this truthfully, that I never allowed myself to dislike a pupil: I never despised stupidity. I saw – you'll smile when you hear me say it, but it's true – every child, stupid and clever alike, as an immortal soul embarked on a mortal pilgrimage. The aim, for stupid and for clever, was to help that soul towards self-awareness. The rewarding aspect of my job was the possibility of the discovery of an enthusiast, for the world pulls itself up, not with the help of its own bootstraps, but with the help of its enthusiasts.

Then my work was suddenly interrupted for two terms by the death of my father. I had to return to settle his affairs and help my mother move into a new home. I came back tired by family affairs, though with renewed energy for my job. Everything seemed exciting, and my interest was awakened whenever I heard my colleagues discussing the children and giving their latest assessment of them.

For some strange reason, Anne seemed to be enjoying a 'bad press' at their hands. These strictures aroused my curiosity. What had she done to deserve their disapproval? When hostile remarks were made about her, I expected someone to rush to her defence;

but no-one did. There were no complaints about her work. That seemed satisfactory enough. But a vague suggestion hung in the air that she was being something of a minx. One of our nicest boys, a cheerful youth called David Nicoll, had gone on to his public school about the time I went on leave. I was told now that he had written to her regularly all last term. That was not a crime, but the implication conveyed to me was that though she had originally encouraged him she was now treating him with scant consideration.

Our second mistress was – and had been for years – the invaluable 'Miss Whit'. Whitworth was her full name. But abbreviations are always favoured in a school. Philippa was 'Miss Pip', and Arthur's other sister Josephine, who taught French, was 'Miss Jo'. I can't tell you what my nickname was, or even if I had one. Miss Whit and I were the complete antithesis of each other in almost every respect. She was a pillar of reliability and punctuality. I showed, all too often, that I regarded time as something for slaves. It is a tribute to Arthur's habitual honesty that, when he was once suggesting to me the advantage of keeping a closer eye on the clock, he added, "I know I'm a bad offender in this respect myself."

It was Miss Whit's duty to prepare the timetable each term, the most thankless task any member of a staff can be allotted. It was always ready when we returned and it was always flawless. She and one of our younger masters stood for punctuality, tidiness and all the prim excellencies, and it was interesting to see how they gravitated towards one another for this very reason. They despised creatures of impulse like myself, who did things on the spur of the moment. Indeed for a long time, I believe that Miss Whit regarded me as something of a humbug, a creature able to discuss educational principles in the drawing-room on Sunday evening but quite unable to get his marks added up in good time for the fortnightly staff-meeting. Distinctly witty, ready to put across a funny story in her native Yorkshire in inimitable fashion, she could no more theorise about education on Sunday evening than she could fly over the moon. Yet in lots of way she was the saviour of the school. I admired the Old Lady and her son for never being bondslaves to the letter of the law, for their ability to make bold decisions, and for admitting frankly their own frequent unpunctualities when rebuking – but oh so tactfully – mine.

Miss Whit was there as a witty and conscientious dogsbody to see that the situation did not get out of hand, to remind Mrs. Hickson of something she had forgotten, and to teach history to the seniors in a way that ensured their getting a good result in School Certificate. With her pince-nez, her great height and her high-necked post-Edwardian blouses, she was a distinctive and almost absurd figure. But her many good qualities earned her our respect and our affection. One day in the staff-room when David Nicoll's name was mentioned and I questioned her as to whether she considered his affections had been trifled with, she endorsed the unfavourable verdict of certain other female members of the staff, who implied that Anne was a breaker of hearts. I demurred. My pupil had never appeared to me a vamp in the making. Her love-hate relationship with Ivor Thomas had the innocence of an affair of the kindergarten.

"Oh you don't notice these things. That young woman knows how to wobble her eyes at the opposite sex."

The devil she did! And what a horrible expression! It is true that I am not good at noticing other persons' emotional involvements, whereas my own, when they occur, go under the microscope. What Miss Whit had said, she had said brusquely and without malice. Rumour in the staff-room with its bogus compassion for the departed Nicoll was already suggesting that he had a successor. It was not impossible. But the Old Lady's vigilance and, still more, her insistence upon ceaseless activity, ensured that we were in no danger ever of becoming a hot-bed of romance. It had taken me two years of patient but steady pleading to persuade the school authorites that the pace was too strenuous and to institute a rest period in the gym after lunch when, stretched on rugs on the floor, the pupils could relax, read, or go to sleep if they liked, while I or one of my colleagues put on a recital of gramophone music for those who wanted to listen. It was a signal victory, long despaired of, and rigorously guarded once it had been secured.

'That young woman knows how to wobble her eyes at the opposite sex.' Perhaps she did. With those eyes, it was not beyond the bounds of possibility. But was it deliberate? To me it seemed that they were all doing her an injustice. What interested me was a definite re-orientation on the part even of Underwood. For a time she had been his star pupil, if it was not an injustice to him to envisage him having such a thing as a star pupil. But now he appeared to be in league with her hostile critics. This was not imagination on my part. Once, when one of those critics had just left the staff-room after some snide reference to her, to which I had raised objection, Underwood, who remained in the room with me, remarked darkly, "You don't know her as well as I do". He did not elaborate, and I made no move towards challenging his contention. I believe in the privacy of the individual, my own and that of others. I never probed. I never invaded the lives of my pupils. I wanted to influence them, but it must be obliquely. I doubt if I have had a heart-to-heart talk with any of them more than half a dozen times in my whole teaching career. I was curious, now, to know why my good-looking, black-haired, saturnine colleague had joined the opposition. He professed to be a misogynist but actually he got on well with our girls, and had a distinct penchant for one pig-tailed, down-right individual called 'Lizzie' Toller, perhaps because she was such a healthy extrovert. At the same time, he had unquestionably been impressed by Anne's elocutionary talent, and it was more than likely that she, for her part, had been impressed by his good looks.

What had happened to explain the change? Something must have, or he would never have made that remark. I knew Underwood pretty well. If there was any rebuff, it must have come from him. Not only was he almost aggressively unsentimental, but he took his professional responsibilities far too seriously to forget them for an instant. What then could have given him this more penetrating insight which he claimed to have, and which, like Miss Whit, he implied that I lacked?

I was not enough interested in the matter to debate it for any length of time. There had been a break, whatever its explanation. If I had been more interested, I might have drawn certain deductions from something said to me by Anne herself a few weeks later. She informed me one day with a definite measure of acerbity, not that ours was a school where they cared nothing for poetry – she could hardly go as far as that – but that there was a certain master in the school who cared nothing for it, and who even openly mocked at it. This master was very plainly Underwood. The charge was a little unfair to him. He did sometimes mock, but only at certain brands of poetry which he personally disliked. He had numerous literary friends, including the Belloc family, and he greatly admired the author of *Ha'nacher Mill*. He was even a poet of sorts himself, and when he produced *The Frogs* of Aristophanes for us as part of the annual school entertainment he had written a verse prologue for it in rhyming couplets which concluded characteristically:-

> So draw the cord and let the curtain rise
> Advance this Planet to these watchers' eyes.
> Courage! And, boldly, though the door be fast
> Peer through the windows that enshrine the Past.
> Be patient, as with mute imploring hand
> We bid you sit through what you cannot stand!

Looking back on it all, I can well imagine that the explanation was a quite simple one. Anne, like other members of her sex in the class, must have seen Underwood as a figure of considerable masculine glamour – an apotheosis to which he was fully entitled – and may have, in an unguarded moment, betrayed her admiration of him, or even expressed it in verse, being much too young to realise that if she wanted his approval she could hardly have taken a more fatal step towards obtaining it. If nothing as crucial as this occurred, it is still possible that his continuous gibes against the over-charged content of the more sentimental sorts of English verse had provoked her one day into a savagely-expressed counter-attack. She was quite capable of it. I could almost hear the biting tones of her riposte. All I knew was that these two were now at logger-heads and that I could not expect to hear either of them singing the praises of the other.

My classes interested me. The previous year I had had the most brilliant senior form in English that it has ever been my privilege to teach, consisting of six or seven girls, all of whom were able, and one or two of whom possessed exceptional ability. Intelligence is infectious; that may seem a strange thing to say, but I have had proof of it. An average talent will rise above itself in association with an exceptional talent. I watched it happen. One brilliant pupil set the standard and before long the others were living up to her. I can give you an idea of the standard when I tell you that, with this group, instead of beginning work on the syllabus for School Certificate a year or even two years before the exam was due, as most schools did, I scorned to so much as open the 'set books' in English until half-way through the Spring term. Though the exam would be taking place in July, I refused to insult them by asking them to step on to the treadmill any earlier. It would only mean covering the ground *ad nauseam*. They could take it in their stride, all of them. And so they did, every one of them securing a Distinction in English.

I had even made them stylists with the help of a little anthology, *Prose of Our Time*. This contained fairly lengthy samples from Lytton Strachey, Blunden, Virginia Woolf, the Sitwells, Percy Lubbock and others. Its editor A.J. Ratcliffe, suggested writing experiments in style on themes similar to those in the extracts he had printed. We made a pact never to analyse or discuss these passages in any way. That would have prevented them from coming to their own understanding of the writer's handling of his subject. I simply read the passage aloud, allowing it to make its own impact. Then I signed to them with finger raised to closed lips to start their imitation. It might be two days before I saw the result. They could prepare a preliminary draft if they wished. They could polish and re-copy. I never stressed that the work was imitative. It was imitation only in manner, not matter. Anyone who conscientiously practises a creative art has at some time done the same. Proust was immensely stimulated by his discovery of Ruskin. Blake confessed that Fuseli was 'damned good to steal from'. Our readings did something of the same sort. At the end of term, and dependent solely on memory, Barbara Westlake did a brief but amazingly successful pastiche of Aldous Huxley's style in *Point Counterpoint*, and the rest came close on her heels with the relatively easier Percy Lubbock and Henry Williamson.

They had all left now. I could hardly expect another class of equally astounding merit. But their successors, though not so outstanding, were very far from being an anticlimax. They were considered to be too young to be a Sixth Form and so were called the Upper Fifth. Anne was one of the five in the form. All forms in the school were relatively small, and the top form was the smallest of all. Their classroom was half-way down the corridor which led to the gymnasium. It was known as the Library, on the strength of the collection of scientific works which had once belonged to Mrs. Arthur's first husband and which filled the glass-fronted compartments of two six-tier sectional bookcases. I am afraid I never once investigated their contents. I realise the importance of biology; I am grateful to science for conferring on us an almost magical extension of vision and hearing; but immediates are not ultimates. I deplore the attitude of dogmatic materialism to the mystery of human consciousness. Are we to believe that an accidental encounter between two gases in an infinitely remote past gave us, after a lengthy period of time during which the principle of natural selection operated unprompted and blindly, that remarkable and complex phenomenon, the author of *Hamlet*? Better to be a 'pagan suckled in a creed outworn' than to use such a gross superstition to explain the underlying and insoluble mystery of our existence here.

All the other class-rooms opened off or were within a few feet of the central dining-hall, but the Library, like the music rooms, was a kind of cultural retreat. I soon stressed this to an even greater degree by adding a massive bookcase to the existent furniture in the room. The school became an indirect gainer by my father's death. In his study was a huge glass-fronted double bookcase of mahogany, with a cupboard below, and a wide ledge running its entire length. To me as a child it was the cultural status-symbol of my adored parent. It was kept locked, but as I grew older, he would occasionally unlock it in my presence and take down and lend me some volume from its shelves. This bookcase now became mine and was despatched to Swanage. By this time I was living in a bungalow out on the school farm. It was distressing to discover that the beaver-board ceiling of the bungalow was altogether too low for the bookcase. With its cupboards, its five tiers of shelves and its carved pediment, it would have projected through the ceiling, if not through the corrugated iron roof. I asked the Old Lady if I might house it in VI A's classroom. It would give the latter a better claim than ever to its title, the Library. And so the great mahogany bookcase moved into a place of honour directly opposite the window. I arranged my own library of books in it, including the eight-volume, vellum-backed, 1908 Stratford edition of Yeats, signed for me by the poet, as well as first editions of a number of other Irish writers, and various books of my father's. I could survey all these treasured possessions as I taught, and I reassured myself that they would be safe under lock and key. I did not think of their situation as a temporary refuge since I had already decided that I would never be likely to find a more suitable professional *pied-à-terre* than the one where I now was. The school allowed me a degree of liberty which it was most unlikely would be available elsewhere. I loved the Dorset landscape. I felt that this English county and the Canton du Vaud in Switzerland were the two places where I felt most 'earthbound', in the best sense of that term; that is to say, linked by some mystical and immemorial quality in my surroundings to the fields, to the very soil.

I was glad to be teaching. I found it the most natural thing in the world to be seated with my elbows spread on a green baize tablecloth and a twelve-year-old standing beside my chair listening to my eloquent abuse of the inadequacy of his or her essay. My contribution to the school may not have been crucial. But it existed – a currant or two in the collective cake, or even, perhaps, a current or two in the general direction of the stream.

In my classes I was aware of a certain subtle difference in my attitudes to the two sexes. I could slate a boy more frankly. If he felt the slating deserved, a boy would not bear me any ill-will. Whereas a girl, if she was in the wrong, would much prefer to think that she had gulled me into believing she was in the right. I sensed that I was implicitly forbidden to part the veils of her self-esteem. But a boy was largely indifferent. Small boys can be cruel. They can take one another into corners to share dark secrets. They can lie brazenly. Nevertheless, deep down in my heart I suspect that the boy is really the finer animal all-round, that he is more generous, cherishes fewer resentments, and is capable of hidden tenderness and sudden heroisms. Equally deep in my heart I am aware that girls can be vulgar and malicious, and can lie as brazenly as any boy. But it was not my business to detect their vulgarities or to intervene in their quarrels. Whereas from time to time one cannot help noticing that they are distinctly picturesque and that, when they choose, they can be charming.

I don't think that my attitude was unfairly influenced by all this. The girls had the advantage. With their wider range in age – from seven to seventeen – there were nearly always one or two whose faces were a pleasure to look at. One ten-year-old was a case in point. Daphne, as I put it in my sonnet, possessed

That infinitesimal more which itself is all
Twixt beauty and beauty missed to delight our sight.

I saw her as a painter might see her. Her face was an arrangement of lovely curves; round brow; high cheek-bones, with the damask-complexioned, flowerlike beauty of certain Russian women. Her rather full underlip, her small nose flattened slightly at the tip, and her almond eyes at once insolent and amused, were full of character. Leggy and coltish, she ran badly, throwing out her legs to the side like many ungainly young things: but she walked like a young goddess and had the smile of a Botticelli angel.

After four o'clock, when tunics were discarded for the rest of the day, she used to wear a brown velvet dress with a narrow round collar of creamy-coloured lace, tied with two long cream ribbons. This was matched with a pair of long brown woollen stockings. Her thick brown curls, divided by a straight line from the centre of her forehead to the nape of her neck, were at last allowed to flow out over her shoulders. She was unpopular with her contemporaries because of a certain arrogance of nature. But when her whole dormitory were in trouble because of some minor nastiness, it was she alone, it turned out, who had held aloof. The dormitory's professed grievance against her was, "She grinds her teeth in her sleep"; a distressing habit, and not an easy one to correct. "Is it really true, Daphne?" I asked her once. She nodded reluctantly, then murmured, "But I can't really help it. I'm asleep and so I don't know I'm doing it."

Daphne was not a complex mystery like David Nicoll's *inamorata*. She was simply a graceful addition to the school scene. I can remember her *début* at her first school dance. There were two dances each term, one at half-term, the other just before we broke up, though in the short spring term we generally omitted the former. The dance was a definite occasion both for the children and the staff. Only the youngest form of all had to forego it. We grumbled of course, coming to it tired by several days of mark-adding, and then by mark-reading in the gym, followed in the afternoon by a speech from the Old Lady to the parents, a function for which one of my colleagues maintained he had to fortify himself with two aspirins. By the time supper was ready, everyone had thawed out and was beginning to feel agreeably festive.

Excitement pervaded the whole building. The girls had started getting their dresses ready as soon as mark-reading was over. The boys pretended indifference, but actually were always the first to assemble in the dining-hall, which, cleared of all its furniture, looked quite like a ballroom. We, the staff, were still in the Raphael finishing our supper. French chalk had been spread on the parquet floor. Two pianos stood side-by-side at one end of the room and for two hours the music master and Miss Whitworth, towering straight-backed on a music-stool beside him, would thump out dance-music for our benefit.

While the staff dawdled over their supper, Daphne and her privileged companions were inspected by Matron. When I first glimpsed her, she was no longer the self-assertive, almost arrogant young woman who had fought so hard earlier in the afternoon to win at musical chairs. Now she suggested ardent yet subdued excitement, an ethereal creature on the threshold of a great event. Even Miss Pip, suspected by us all of preferring small boys – she helped with the Cubs – had softened towards the admiring band of small girls who gathered round her on occasions like this; and, when I came into the hall, she was standing in front of Daphne, laughing and complimenting her upon her dress, a party frock of pink muslin in a series of flounces, sleeveless and collarless save for a border of tiny embroidered roses.

I danced with colleagues, with an occasional parent but chiefly with the children. Daphne refused me; she was too shy, and she was gone before the first Paul Jones, where chance might have over-ruled her reluctance. Though I was entranced by her lithe beauty, I was, as I told you, very much on my guard lest she should seem to enjoy my special favour. In the classroom I used to snub her with; "Don't chew your upper lip," or "If you can't do better than this, I shall have to send you back to Miss Pip's class." She must never know that she was a favourite, or that I was secretly flattered when she summoned me, by banging with her right hand on the cloth, to sit beside her at one of the long tables at tea, even though I was perfectly aware that it was because I didn't eat the two pieces of toast provided for the staff and invariably gave them to my neighbour.

To get back to my new senior form. Of the five who had come up at the beginning of the new school year to constitute it, all were fairly talented. Anne was unquestionably the most interesting, and her classmates would have endorsed this opinion. It was accepted that her chief talent lay in music. She had no pretensions to being a blue-stocking. Nor did I ever think of her as one. I thought of her more as a personality. The curious thing was that, now that I found myself at last teaching her English, we quarrelled frequently.

Maybe some similarity in temperament made us strike what were relatively amicable sparks out of each other. Or is it possible that I made a false start? Quite early I complained,

"You can write quite well when you're on your own ground. But you can't be bothered to make the effort if it's something which lies outside your own interests."

"Why do you expect me to be good?" she replied, in her rather teasing voice. "I don't want to be a writer."

"Well, even so, you may one day wish to write your memoirs as a musician. I want them to be well written."

I called it just now her teasing voice. But that is not quite the correct term. Persuasive might be a better word. I know I referred earlier to a certain satiric note in her voice. But a person can have two voices. Indeed many voices. The overtones of Anne's were as characteristic as anything in the whole of her composition. They were like a signpost pointing in the direction of a destination still many miles away.

Her literary ancestry made me raise my sights where her work was concerned. I saw a good deal of her parents. They fetched her on Saturday, brought her back on Sunday and often, as I've said, stayed for the concert. She became more explicable in terms of these two cultured individuals. They had endowed her with their own sensibility and seemed a little worried at the thought of the distress it might occasion her.

"He thinks me stupid," she told her mother in front of me one Sunday evening. "When he taught me Latin in the Fourth he was reduced to hitting me on the head with a book." "What a lie, Anne!" I had to exclaim, "I've never hit anyone on the head with a book since I've been here." But she was convinced that it had happened. We argued the point fiercely, and I began to wonder could I ever have flipped her lightly with the cover of her own exercise book. No-one, least of all a schoolmaster, sees himself as others see him.

In class, now that I taught her English, her comments were sometimes characteristically sardonic. They touched everything but poetry. Only poetry was holy. For the first time in my life, I found I had met someone to whom it seemed as important and as unique as it had to me as a boy. It and religion were bracketed for me as the two most important things in the world. They appealed to the same depths. I suppose I inherited this attitude from my parents, as Anne did from hers. Her response affected my whole attitude to my new class. Whenever I read a poem aloud, I seemed to be as much aware of this pupil's sensibility as of my own. Poetry was magic. It was the language not merely of the Muses, but of the gods. Long after he has written a poem, a poet may say to himself, "Whatever made me think of that?", or "What could have given me that exact phrase?" It seems to him that he must momentarily have experienced a different kind of consciousness, and that something has heated his mental and emotional – and verbal – processes and made them incandescent. No effort of will could ever have achieved what, in the outcome, reads to him now so easily and inevitably.

It is plain from this that, though we quarrelled, I welcomed her presence in the class. The others showed interest in the work, but she was a sounding-fork which one could bring into use to test a particular poem. If its lines were in tune with her vibrations, then all was well.

Any humiliations she may have suffered at my hands while learning Latin were now atoned for. Cortot was giving a Chopin recital in Bournemouth Pavilion and I obtained permission to take Anne and three other equally musical pupils to it. At the last minute there was a complication. It was Underwood's free after-noon and he enquired whether he might accompany us. I was delighted to have him, the only colleague with whom I had any real cultural accord. But I dreaded the effect of his astringent tongue on at least one member of the party.

In the end, I decided it was better to try and forestall what might happen. At breakfast – for I breakfasted at the school – I said to Anne:

"Mr. Underwood is coming with us this afternoon. That will be nice. But you're not to listen to him if he becomes condemnatory. We spoil things for people by crabbing them. Don't worry about what you disapprove or dislike in life. Just remain silent about it. Our judgements are never final, and in any case it is a mistake to dwell on our dislikes. It only encourages a negative attitude to things."

My homily was directed as much to the absent Underwood as to her; though I would not have dared subject him to it. I need not have worried. In the end the warning turned out to be unnecessary. The whole expedition was a success from the moment we set off and cycled past the little tin Methodist chapel in its dour isolation amongst trees in the lane taking us to the Studland road. Passing through the gap between Ballard and Nine Barrow Down, so familiar to me from my morning rides, we climbed the hill skirting the steep green slopes of the local golf course and ran down towards a copse of pines with pink-flushed trunks that marked the turning to the ferry road. When we reached the wooden toll gate, the attendant came out from his hut, collected our fares, opened the gate for us, and we cycled across the three miles of open, heather-covered moorland which led to the steam ferry bridging the narrow channel that gave access to Poole Harbour. Both road and ferry were a private venture of the Banks family, and must have given them a richer return than any investment they had ever made, for it saved twelve miles on the alternative route to Bournemouth. It was used not only by countless cars but by the Swanage-Studland bus a number of times each day.

I elaborate all this, I suppose, for the satisfaction of living it again. For sixty years the ferry had been pulling itself backwards and forwards across the quarter of a mile of narrow strait through which, for some strange reason, there flow four rapid tides each day.

When we arrived at the ferry a bus and a number of cars were already in place. We wheeled our bicycles on board and went up to the tiny upper deck to admire the view, not only out to sea but also north to the low wooded profile of Brownsea Island which concealed the unsightliness of Poole with its blackened brick chimneys. After the ferry there followed four miles of cycling past private houses belonging to wealthy individuals, set well back from the road and embedded in the Bournemouth pines, until we came to the sea-front and to the concert pavilion. There Cortot, like a frail pale-visaged archangel, played in such a way that even Underwood could not fault him. Years later I would meet Cortot, and would ask him how he managed to render his favourite composer with such unique understanding. "I try to be Chopin!" was his reply. At Bournemouth, he certainly made us feel that something of the sort was happening. We emerged into the public gardens silenced by the magic of a great artist. As we rode home, one at least of the party had the feeling of being calmed in spirit. At first our mood was that of a Chopin nocturne, but before we got back it had given way to one of elation and laughter, thanks to all the exercise the afternoon had given us.

A few days later something happened which fundamentally affected my attitude to Anne. I knew this at the time. It is a little difficult to explain, even for someone who spends his life trying to explain himself to himself. While some people try to observe and analyse everything, others move through life from action to action, guided by impulse or firmly-rooted resolution. A vast number of intermediate types rush frantically towards some ready-made solution which they find reassuring, just as a drowning man clutches gratefully at a floating hen-coop.

How different are the introverts; who spend much of their time wondering not merely who they are, but what they are! It is probably to satisfy these interrogators of life that the whole edifice of literature has arisen. Some law of their being decrees that in books they will find certain welcome inklings of underlying truth.

This is a little much to expect. All the same, we expect it. And, if disappointment awaits us, there is generally a consolation prize of some sort to make amends. For the answers proffered to our queries, although they may not be true, can be worded so felicitiously as to suggest that they hold a grain or two of truth. No-one has explained our response to music, and yet we have all listened to a piece of music and felt that it was making some distinct revelation of truth to us. And in the same way, arrangements of words can cast a spell over us, simply because they appear to be weighted with overtones which satisfy a deep longing in our puzzled souls. The cadences of such passages unite with our being. Language has ceased to be language and has become a form of vibrant thought.

I am going to give you an example of this. You know Shelley's sonnet 'Mutability'? No? Well it is very far from being one of his best efforts, but it happened to be the opening item in a selection of his work prescribed for study in the course which the top form were doing for their certificate the following July. The sonnet is not great poetry:-

We are as clouds that veil the midnight moon;
    How restlessly they speed, and gleam, and quiver,
Streaking the darkness radiantly! – yet soon
    Night closes round, and they are lost for ever: . . .

After which very tame beginning, Shelley proceeds to draw a parallel between these drifting clouds and our own changing states of mind where 'a dream has power to poison sleep', or 'one wandering thought pollutes the day'.

It is fustian stuff. But there it was, confronting us on page one of the book, and in the hardness of my heart I directed the five figures gathered round the table in the Library to write me a paraphrase of it.

They groaned in spirit, grumbled a little, then opened their exercise books and began to write.

"Are you ready?" I asked them, presently.

"No, not quite."

"You can have five minutes more. Then we'll read them aloud."

The view from the classroom window was not an inspiring one. It looked out across a strip of tired grass at the back of the dining hall towards the kindergarten, behind which rose the steel framework of the generator, that miniature Eiffel Tower with its wheel revolving briskly and noisily in the sunlight. If the wind got up too much the school carpenter, or his son, or even Arthur himself would have to rush out, seize an iron crank and swing the wide rudder apparatus round to a different angle, throwing the wheel out of action and averting possible disaster. What was needed was wind, but not too much.

I told them to stop writing and to pass their books to Joan Wilson to read aloud. I made it a rule in all my classes to try to judge work of this kind as far as possible anonymously. If one knows who the writer is, there is always the danger that one starts with an expectation of either good or bad achievement. But that is not fair. I much preferred to weigh my verdict with a completely unbiassed mind.

What I heard read on this occasion was no more than moderately good. Only when Joan reached the last of the paraphrases did I prick up my ears. I have that paraphrase still. If you wait a minute I will read it to you. I have kept the exercise book.

Mutability

"Humanity is like a mass of clouds, that are lighted up and that streak the darkness of night with radiance. And yet how soon the night again swallows them up and they are engulfed in darkness. And it is like music played with lyres in forgotten ages, which bring no second note like the last but all are different. When we sleep a mere dream can poison our rest; or when we get up our thoughts can stain our lives. We jump lightly from thinking to reasoning, from laughing to crying, overwhelm ourselves with self-pity, or cast away all our troubles and are utterly carefree. But whatever happens it is the same. For the path of our departure from us is free, be it joy or sorrow. Nothing lives on but the fickleness of the world; that is – Mutability!"

When she had finished reading, I cried out, "Well done! Well done someone! I call that really good. Whose is it?" "It's Anne's." "Bravo, Anne. That's the best thing I've ever had from you."

I had been slating her consistently about her English, and now she leaped suddenly into favour. You will ask what was there in any way exceptional about the passage. It pleased me because of the spontaneous ease with which it seemed to have found each phrase. To me there was far more melancholy in Anne's prose version than in Shelley's fourteen lines. She had caught the essence of his mood and given it cadenced rebirth. Shelley's idea seemed to need the simplicity of prose rather than the corseted restriction of iambic pentameters. Her paraphrase had for me the finality of Callimachus's epitaph on his friend Charidas:- "O Charidas, what of the underworld? Much darkness. And the resurrection? A lie. And Pluto? A fable. We perish." Her paraphrase was as direct as the clipped speech of that Greek epigram.

I picked up the exercise books from the table and looked with studied carelessness at the top one in the pile. The book was almost full. There were only a few unused pages at its end. I would forget to give it back to her. She could get a new one. The old one deserved a better fate than to be gathered up by the lame Cuffey and used to re-light the boiler the next time Matron came storming down to say that there was no hot water. The paraphrase by its simplicity and a certain deliberate or accidental note of finality delighted me. It revealed a natural and unconscious sense of rhythm. I still have it. I see you are smiling to think that I have kept it all these years, but I offer no apology.

In the days that followed Anne seemed tired, and more silent than usual. If she spoke, one was more likely to hear that biting inflexion in her voice than the musical resonance of her happier moments. Endless rehearsals for the annual school play were taking it out of her. She looked pale and wretched. It was doubtful if her class got to bed early enough to get the sleep they needed. She admitted to being chronically tired. Thursday was one of the two days on which I presided at the children's tea. I happened to notice her at a table nearby as the meal was ending. I seldom spoke intimately to the children and then only when I felt – by a kind of instinct – that the right moment had come. On this occasion, I was prompted by such an impulse and obeyed it.

Only about half-a-dozen children remained at the tables and the maids were beginning to clear. I called Anne across to me. "Sit down." She sat in the place of another child who had left. "You look tired." "I am tired, and so bad-tempered. Everything maddens me." "Well, the holidays are coming." "Yes, but I'm so irritable at home. And people always seem to be on top of me. And I'm so beastly to them." "I am irritable myself and can sympathise with you. You must just study your machine and handle it better. You are cross because you are tired; and you are tired because you don't know the moment to stop. When one feels like that, the best thing is to get away from people, to be alone for a bit. Persons of your temperament need plenty of solitude. But it takes strength of mind to secure it, to go for a long walk alone, to abandon whatever is fussing us and be passive for a bit. Anyone like us spends themselves freely and needs time as it were to re-charge the battery of their life. You mustn't expect to live always on the crest of the wave, and you must just study how to deal with your moments of depression and boredom."

I cannot remember what else I said to her. But I said enough to convince her that her troubles were by no means unique, that they were shared and experienced by lots of other people. And this alone, as I knew myself, was an aid. To a certain extent I was only passing on advice that the Old Lady had given me on several occasions. The cups and saucers clattered; the maids moved quickly about the room, collecting the crockery; the few remaining children got up and left, until finally only Anne and myself and one little boy, notorious for his slowness, were left. I looked at that pale, beautiful face, with its brown hair drawn back from the white, rounded forehead, and I thought, "Yes, you are of the select. But what does that mean? It means that you are going to suffer. Because you feel things more acutely you will relish them more, but your moments of despair are going to be trebled too. You will not go through life immunised against its sorrow by dosages of stupidity or levity, or because you have managed to make yourself primly defensive against all its possible barbs. You will savour its good moments and see its loveliness. But what has it to say to you? What has it to say to us all?"

And, looking up from the table I noticed outside on the terrace someone who, because she was not temperamental, or because she concealed temperament so successfully, might almost have been the text of my homily. It was Mrs. Arthur; one of the least hurried persons I have ever met. Although she was never idle, although her flat in the attic was liable to invasion at any time, and three children and a lady-nurse were now helping to fill it, she pursued all her objectives with a serenity which suggested complete leisure, performing every action of her life so calmly, so peacefully that she might be living in a dream or in eternity. She was the point of rest at the centre of the school-hurricane. It cannot have been easy for her to live in such a din of contending voices. But she accepted it. All her fires were buried deep in her self-controlled nature.

There was a curious sequel to this incident at the tea-table. Anne went home as she always did for the week-end. It was her unique privilege, granted because of her special music lessons. When she returned on Sunday evening, her mother came with her and remained for the concert. I had a few words with her when it was over. She told me that Anne had arrived home and had said, "I thought he knew nothing about me but he understands me better than anyone else in the world." Our five minutes' conversation while the maids were clearing tea had given me this undeserved renown. Her mother was grateful to me for having helped her. She knew that one accepts from strangers what one would reject if it came from a mere parent.

A few days after the reading of the paraphrase I redeemed a promise by unlocking the great bookcase which had come to me under my father's will. By then the class had had several weeks to contemplate with curiosity its locked contents. They gathered round and I noticed that curiosity, or perhaps politeness, made them begin by investigating the few copies of my own books which were to be found on one of the shelves. Anne took down a volume of poems, opened it at random, and presently asked indignantly, "What do you mean? I don't understand. How can one love too much?" Her eye had caught an eight-line poem entitled 'He who loves beauty wisely'.

> He who loves beauty wisely
> Loves her least touch.
> She can scourge him with arrows
> Who loves too much;
> Who turns aside, who lingers,
> Who leaves the throng,
> She can scourge him with scorpions
> Who loves too long.

If I had had time to consider, I might have said, "My poem only means that if one loves unhappily or unsuccessfully, without being loved in return, one can be made very wretched. I do not of course mean that it is ever foolish to love one person for a long time." But I was hurried and a little taken aback by the astonishment in her voice. And so, instead, I said, "People are made very unhappy, as you know, by love. They can even kill themselves in despair, put their heads in gas ovens, as you read in the papers. This is because they have lost their sense of proportion; they have not remained masters of their own minds. We must never surrender so completely to our emotions that we are helpless against them. If we do, we lay ourselves open to being very, very unhappy."

I had missed her point. She thought I meant that love should always be ephemeral, a very different conception from her own on that subject. In a poem of hers, discovered at the back of one of her exercise books, I found her affirming, with almost the arrogance of Yeats, that love outlasts the stars. Yeats had said it more effectively than a schoolgirl could do:-

> Time drops in decay,
> Like a candle burnt out,
> And the mountains and woods
> Have their day, have their day;
> What one in the rout
> Of the fire-born moods
> Has fallen away?

But she had endorsed his contention.

Exploration of the contents of the great bookcase kept them occupied for a whole period. When Anne drew out a volume of my poems printed in Paris with hand-coloured *pochoir* decorations by a French artist, I had to tell her; "That's out of print. But there's a later book which includes all the poems and a lot more as well, and which I can give you if you remind me some time." Then, feeling I had broken my rule of never seeming to differentiate between my pupils, I added to the other four; "I can't do the same for everyone, though I have enough of another little book – sonnets, which I doubt you'll understand – but if you like, I will give you that." They expressed their gratitude and I thought to myself, "One more of your facile promises to sting your wretched conscience with periodic qualms until it is fulfilled; if ever it is fulfilled!"

The days of the term slipped by imperceptibly, and almost before we realized it rehearsals for the school play were upon us. The school play entailed endless dressmaking for the older girls who had to make their own costumes, and for Miss Arnold who elected to paint the gigantic backcloth on a huge canvas laid out flat on the floor in her studio. Engaged on these labours, she would swathe her head in the nearest thing to a Victorian turban that I have ever seen outside a Dickens illustration. This gallant soul, with her nasal, chronically-adenoidal intonation, and a sense of fun which had accompanied her into what must have been her early sixties, was very much a part of the school. At the end of term concert, just as one could count on Arthur's baritone for "Friend o'Mine" and "Trumpeter, what are you sounding now?", or on Hobhouse for the recitation of one of Hillaire Belloc's cautionary tales, so she had a contribution which was an invariable request item upon the programme – the plea of the excited lady in a department store who wishes to purchase "two dozen double-damask dinner napkins". For years it was a popular item in the repertoire of a well-known music-hall comedienne, yet it was hard to believe that she could have made any more of it than our elderly art mistress, whose nasal disability greatly multiplied the incredible series of variations and ever-increasing distortions wrung from that one simple phrase, "two dozen double-damask dinner napkins". Her recitation was always a howling success.

I liked Miss Arnold, I had always liked her. But it is strange how a quite slight and accidental remark can send someone, suddenly, up in our estimation. I was delighted when she said at supper one Sunday after a literary programme to which Anne had contributed, "How pretty that girl looked when she was reciting this evening." Of course Anne was pretty. I had always know it. But the heroic old scene-painter, by this chance testimonial, suddenly soared in my opinion. I saw her not merely as the amusing and much-appreciated colleague, which she had always been, but as a person of taste and discrimination.

Perhaps that remark was a factor in prompting me to keep my promise of the book. It is impossible to dissect a situation after a number of years; and I would have found it even harder at the time. You see, I believe our emotions carry us along in much the same way as a train does. At one moment we look out of the window and see a quiet field or a copse of larches. But if, five minutes later, anyone were to ask us about that field we could tell them practically nothing, for that field has been succeeded by a river, and the river by a stretch of country, the tumbled nature of which has almost slipped from memory. All we can assert for certainty is that we set out from one point and presently arrived at another. And I can't tell you that even. I am not certain when or where this particular journey began or if it even had an ending. I suppose the nearest thing to one would be this moment now, when I am telling you this story.

I mustn't mislead you. Certain landmarks do stand out. I am coming to one. I had promised Anne a book. But it took me at least three weeks to implement my promise, which shows that I wasn't unduly preoccupied with the obligation.

Finding her alone in the library one afternoon before tea, I said to her, "By the way, I must give you that book." I unlocked the lower cupboard-portion of the book-case and soon found what I was looking for. It was the work of a moment or two to inscribe it, "To Anne who cares for poetry." "There you are!" She was reading the inscription as I turned away. I could see her face light up radiantly with an expression of deep pleasure. I was standing with my back to her, opening the upper part of the bookcase for a book needed for my next class, when I heard her exclaim "Oh, I must kiss you!" She made a quick movement towards me and her hands were already on my shoulders before I could say, "Oh, no! It wouldn't do at all! I should lose my job at once if my pupils took to kissing me."

At the time I had little doubt that this was the right reaction to her words. I was surprised and taken aback by her sudden, warm-hearted impulsiveness. It might have been better to have accepted the kiss as the entirely natural expression of the gratitude of a young girl to someone twice her age. But I did not look at it that way. I was not expecting it, so I was neither flattered, nor even pleased, only amazed. I got what I wanted, locked the bookcase, put the labelled key back in my pocket, and turned to go. What had I done? Her action had been so entirely spontaneous that it seemed ridiculous that I should have suppressed it. I had checked it; rationalised it; coldly reduced it to its proper place in the scheme of school life; in fact I had only just stopped short of humiliating her. I did not think this at the time; but I feel it now. For the briefest second she seemed a little crestfallen; then she renewed her thanks for the book. And before we left the Library she said slowly, as though she had been thinking the matter over, "Yes, perhaps you are right about the kiss."

This incident was a landmark. It was something definitely different from anything seen previously from the train. You could say that it changed my whole attitude to her. I remember being told once by someone that a priest in the confessional, if a girl tells him that she has been kissed, will cross-examine her as to the nature of the kiss. Was it given light-heartedly, in a mood of laughter and affection, or was it passionate and prolonged? It seems funny that priests should have to constitute themselves an authority upon the nature of kisses. But here was I worrying about a kiss which had not even been given. I suppose the very fact that it was non-existent gave it – like unicorns, or water-nymphs, or dryads – all the greater power over the imagination. Certainly it did something to me far beyond what it had any legitimate right to do. I have a fair measure of assurance. But fundamentally I am shy. It is not the audacious who are most susceptible; it is the shy. For they live in a world in which evaluations tend to be rated at the highest level. Of course kisses can be graded. There are those which mean next to nothing, or absolutely nothing. A peck on the cheek, dutifully rendered is scarcely a kiss at all. I have known a woman friend, departing for Australia, demand a farewell kiss from me, and, when it was given say, "Do you call that a kiss?" And I knew she was right. But it was her own fault. She had been paid in false coin since no real currency was available. An ungiven kiss from a young girl can prove to be in a different category altogether. It may be wealth in much the same way that a promissory note or a post-dated cheque can be called wealth.

Something had occurred which gave our whole relationship a different aspect. I had always been aware of the fact that Anne was pretty. That had not needed Miss Arnold's endorsement to establish it. Now I was made permanently conscious of the fact. She had beautifully-curved eyebrows, a fine forehead and nose, and a wide mouth. For the first time I became fully aware how wonderful her eyes were; huge, limpid, child-like and slightly reproachful, as though saying, "Take care. I have learnt already that everything beautiful in life has also the power to hurt." When she looked at one like this, it was as though she was on the point of wincing at something. At what? At the unknown. At the thought of humanity, that mass of clouds which streaks the night for the moment with radiance and then is engulfed in darkness?

It is a long time ago and you may feel that I am constructing what I am telling you now out of my imagination. But I do not think that this is so. For one thing I noted much of it in my journal at the time. And anything once set down on paper, even if we leave it unread, has successfully dodged extinction. It is as though our over-soul – to use Paul Brunton's expression – said to us, "So you think this was to some degree crucial?"; or, "What happened then became an integral part of your essential self?"; or, merely, "So you decided at the time that it was worth taking a mental photograph of the occasion?" I do not say that I would answer "Yes" to any of these three questions. But what I can say is that I am not inventing. I am not exaggerating. What I tell you did take place.

For several days after the incident, I continued to think of her paraphrase. It confirmed my conviction that I had someone in my form whose response to literature not only went deeper than that of her companions, but who had the gift of words, of unconsciously shaping a phrase to fit a thought, of liberating the soul from silence. The same was even more true now of the proferred kiss. It made her different in kind from her fellows.

We were still pursuing Shelley along his ethereal and labyrinthine pathways. Anne sat on my right at the table and whenever anything more than usually musical or evocative was read, I would look up from my book to see how that particular line had affected her, knowing that, if I did, our eyes were fairly certain to meet in mutual approval. I began to feel that I was almost on the threshold of understanding her. Always, before, I had seen her from outside. I had admired her, but quite impersonally. Now it was as if I began to see her from within. I would look forward to a lesson if she was to be there. It pleased me to come upon her down at the farm, in dungarees, painting wagons with Brimacombe's "farm class". Or I might find her turning the wheel of the chaff-cutter, or sawing wood with a cross-saw. Sometimes she was in the group which I took myself for these activities, and it was pleasant to see her laughing, teasing her companions, and shedding every sign of melancholy as we worked. She might accompany me to the forge when one of the horses unexpectedly needed a shoe, sitting her mount bareback and glad of an opportunity for a ride. I had had other delightful pupils, many of them, but here was one who had the strange distinction of making me feel that she was unique.

For that matter so were our surroundings. They were rural and yet within five minutes' walk of the little seaside town which had been growing in favour with discriminating people since the beginning of the century. By buying agricultural land on the very outskirts of Swanage while it was still obtainable, the Old Lady had saved the situation. We lived in a dual society. The three or four farm hands, the school carpenter and his son were as much a part of the community as anyone. Our school numbers would be considered minute today. They were between seventy and eighty. But, as that fellow Schumacher has been saying, 'small is beautiful'. And the landscape! Bounty from le Bon Dieu! My bungalow stood in a great field which had run wild for ten years, the builder who had cast lustful eyes on it having found that clients would not risk a site reached by a chalk track across muddy land. So he disposed of it. Huge bulwarks of prodigal gorse extended out from a distant hedge, flooding the air with their sweetness. They made a paradise for small birds. Brimacombe, our farm manager, fresh from his agricultural college, was relentless in his determination to eradicate them but they were still there. And across this gorse brake one looked upwards towards the rhythmic easy-flowing line of Nine Barrow Down at the back of Godlinstone with its great meadow traversed by the narrowest and most minute of streams. The slow curve of the down was like a forearm of slumbering Mother Earth. And in the evening light, against a

sky of saffron or egg-shell green, it achieved a saliency equal to
that of those great granite ridges one sees against a cerulean
background in the Alps. But the effect of the down was more
calming, more harmonious, and, as the light faded, its outline
became darker and more magical and a sense of infinite peace
accompanied the dusk. You had only to look at it to become
convinced that one's diagnosis of the human situation was wrong,
and that all our dreads and apprehensions are false since, in
actual fact, Nature loves us.

I was not the only creature to approve that spot. Two years
running, I saw in exactly the same place, not far from the enamel-
led bath used as a water trough for the horses, a small bird, little
larger than a starling, with a mobile, fawn-coloured head and
bright eyes. It arrived towards the beginning of June, and for
thirty-six hours it rested, or walked about the grass, a yard in this
direction, a yard in that, exactly as though it had staked a claim on
that tiny area twelve months before. There was no cover nearer
than the adjoining hedge, but it did not seem to mind. It
appeared tired and a little dazed. If I went too near it flew into the
hedge. It was a turtle-dove. It had made itself the absentee land-
lord of those few square yards of Dorset soil. And, returning
annually to have a glance over its property before continuing its
migration northwards, it made me wonder if our departed spirits
will one day feel much the same about some corner of earth.

A whole host of similar memories are linked to the school's
setting. In summer I was free to take my classes out of doors
whenever I liked, reading in the sandpit, while a corn-crake
provided us with off-stage noises in the nearby hayfield, or
adjourning to the tiny 'farm garden' which consisted of a scented
elder-bush, a few lilacs, a single flower-bed, and a triangular
patch of mown grass sloping up from the big green-house at the
back of the ancient farmhouse, roofed with huge centuries-old
slabs of Purbeck stone in place of slates. I have known half a dozen
girls fling themselves down on that triangle of grass and plead,

"Can we take our stockings off?"

"I suppose so."

They undid their suspenders with discretion and lightning
celerity and whipped off six pairs of long black stockings; we were
now free to turn our attention to Keats and to his evocative
nightingale.

Perhaps this rural setting meant more to me than it did to my pupils, many of whom, like Anne, came from the very heart of Dorset. I don't know what she thought of it. I never cross-examine the young on their reactions to life. My own privacy of mind is so precious to me that I could not dream of invading that of another. One may give oneself away by handfuls in one's books, very much as I am doing now, but it is being done object-ively, and only after a lapse of time has allowed me to put myself outside the events and emotions. I would have found it absolutely impossible to discuss what was happening to me in connection with this pupil with even the closest friend at the time when it was happening. To use that absurd and untrue cliché, "I would have died first." Of course, I would not have died; nor would anyone who uses the silly phrase. I have always found life much too interesting. But if you had questioned me then you would have been met with contemptuous silence. What was happening to me? I didn't know what was happening to me. Perhaps I didn't want to know. The very most I knew was that something was happening.

I hesitated to ask myself if I loved The Pupil. I am, I know, self-conscious by nature; but I abhor any dramatization of a situation. I prefer to underestimate it. Only self-indulgent per-sonalities wish to see their emotions file before them in a kind of shoddy parade. They find it reassuring. "Actually yes, actually, I felt this", or, "no doubt about it, I felt that". And down it goes, stressed to a degree that quickly warps the truth into falsehood. Whereas where suffering is concerned, the only acceptable course to me has always seemed Lionel Johnson's precept of silence:

I have not spoken of these things
Save to one man and to God.

Is the one man necessary? God would have been enough. Is even God necessary? The Almighty has enough on his hands already without being troubled with the details of rejected affec-tion.

At the time it would have seemed to me silly and melodramatic to declare to man or God, "I love Anne". Such a pronouncement could even have been untrue. It was a different thing to admit to myself, and only to myself, that I was *in love* with her. Reviewing the whole episode now I realize that of course I was in love with her, and for the very best of reasons; that is for no reason at all. This surrender to the irrational is at the very core of that mysterious condition which we term "being in love". The mere sight of someone has become to us an inestimable boon. Argued in a court of law an advocate would feel that he had no case at all. How can one establish that a person is in love, when all the evidence is so slender, so shadowy, so hypothetical? Yet the lover knows that he is guilty of the charge. He has betrayed the fact in a dozen trivial details, not one of which, in itself, may be sufficient to establish his offence beyond all reasonable doubt.

And is it a crime? Is it a crime to wish anyone great happiness? Is it a crime to be concerned for their safety? Is it a crime to feel, as one listens to someone, "No-one else could have made that remark with just that almost imperceptible inflexion which takes it out of the commonplace?"

I never doubted that I had fallen in love. It was not the first time and it would not be the last. But it would have seemed absolutely inconceivable to me that I should express that love, verbally or in any other way. It was not passion. It was not disguised instinct. It was not hallucination, any more than Beethoven's hinted love for one favoured pupil had been hallucination. It was reality. Beethoven had turned his "reality" into a sonata, thus achieving a relative emancipation of spirit from something which had held him enslaved for weeks. Love is, as I have probably said already, the discovery of an unsuspected and exceptional value in a particular individual. And it may, of course, find its natural expression in sexual tenderness. But not necessarily so. How much tenderness was there between Dante and Beatrice? Between Petrarch and Laura? Between Yeats and Maud Gonne?

It is this distinction between two linked elements to which our epoch tends to remain so obstinately blind. Like the writer who said, "Take eloquence and wring its neck," a whole generation – demanding nothing of their authors except that they should shock – has said "Take romance and wring its neck." One can of course notice a complete stranger, some rounded and personable member of the opposite sex, and think fleetingly, "How pleasant to be invited to bed by you!" But such anonymous and momentary craving is simply part of an accepted, and as quickly rejected, physical urge. But an obsession with the *persona* of another individual is an altogether different thing. That my feelings about

Anne were wholly innocuous only made the preoccupation all the more baffling and perhaps all the more compelling. She must have had some inkling of her mysterious gift. It was an affirmation of potentiality, a prophetic insistence made in complete innocence: "I am capable of love and you must surely see that."

Sometimes I ask myself, "Was she beautiful? Was that the explanation?" But I know that it was not. In a sense she was beautiful; but not notably so. An onlooker merely observing her in a group of youthful contemporaries would have been unlikely to pick her out. There was her fine forehead. But fine foreheads are no great rarity. Even her mannerisms were ones unlikely to attract attention. She might read Shakespeare with penetrating emotion, but her normal speaking voice, as I had noticed so often and have already mentioned, had that astringent quality, as though she were biting her own words in condemnation of the line of thought which they had just taken.

Strangely I find it much easier to recall her voice than her appearance, that crystal-clear voice with its sardonic inflexions. Her appearance evades me. As a popular Edwardian cliché put it – very much in the same mood as the songs of the period by Tosti and others – "The eyes are the window of the soul." It is a truism, yet it has its elements of profundity. Anne's eyes were the windows of her soul. But what was much more significant was that they made you realise she had a soul. Even as singers in an opera furnish us with an immediate reminder of our own latent potential of human ardour, overlaid daily by the settling dust of trivialities, so, in the same way, contact with Anne tended to re-kindle a part of one's essential nature which seemed in danger of suffering extinction.

I have a feeling all the time that I am defending a position; and even at times counter-attacking. People today see "love" merely as the emotional trimmings of a physiological urge. That won't do. The poet Yeats put the matter in a nutshell when he made his "Woman Young and Old" hold such persons up to scorn.

> Flinging from his arms I laughed
> To think his passion such
> He fancied that I gave a soul
> Did but our bodies touch,
> And laughed upon his breast to think
> Beast gave beast as much.

I am not advocating a return to the sublimated unrealities of Victorian sentiment. But if the human spirit comes into it at all, let us admit the fact and not reduce "love" to the level of a pressing physical need. Plato believed that one of the indications of love should be a desire to nourish the loved one upon all that is best and truest in human thought. I'm going to give you an illustration of that now.

I have plenty of selfishness in my composition. It betrays itself in a variety of ways. I revealed it even in what I was willing to share with my pupils. I kept my most treasured predilections to myself as being too hallowed to endanger. I could not risk their desecration by the insensitive or the stupid. When I read something aloud to them at one of my concerts on Sunday evenings, I would often say, "Listen to this!" or "I'll be very surprised if you don't like what I'm going to give you now." But, like Ananaias, who kept back half the purchase price of his field, I never gave them that which I valued most of all. It might result in its devaluation in my own spiritual currency.

That autumn I broke with my rule. I told the form in the Library that once a week we would have a class which would not be a class in the ordinary sense of the term at all.

"If your work has been good, we will do something different on Thursdays, in the period after tea and before your dancing lesson. I'll devote it to reading to you great literature, but literature which has absolutely nothing to do with your course."

Though I made the announcement with an air of deliberate informality, I was perfectly aware that what I was doing I was doing for the sake of one pupil. When the second Thursday came I introduced a further innovation, and we moved from the table to sit around the class-room fire. I wanted things to be like this. I wanted the occasion to avoid even the faintest hint of academic motivation.

They had changed out of their school tunics into whatever frock they preferred. This was part of their daily routine. Anne sat on the floor; the other four drew their chairs into a half-circle in front of the grate. I won't trouble you with a recital of what the readings were, but they ranged from Jean Richepin's "Song of Mary of the Angels" and Flecker's "To a Poet a Thousand Years Hence", to Synge's play *Deirdre of the Sorrows*, and to that sublime flight of Socratic patience and dignity, *The Apology*. Why, I wonder, do those four examples present themselves in memory now? They are all concerned with death. Perhaps some unacknowledged or banished element in my nature accounts for this. It was an instinctive choice, but it matched my immediate response to the sadness implicit in the Mutability paraphrase. We were hearing a lot about "sharing" from the so-called Oxford Group. I enjoyed this literary "sharing" as much as any of Buchman's converts appeared to enjoy "sharing" their often very trivial misdemeanours. It was a privilege to be able to chant Deirdre's farewell to her and Naisi's Scottish refuge:- "Woods of Cuan, woods of Cuan. It's seven years we've had a life was joy only and this day we're going west, this day we're facing death maybe, and death should be a poor untidy thing, though it's a queen that dies." And later, when they have been betrayed and are to pay with their lives for their return from exile, I enjoyed her marvellous rebuke to those who quarrel about the situation which she has accepted:- "Draw back a little with the squabbling of fools . . . I have put away sorrow like a shoe that is worn out and muddy. . . . It is not a small thing to get rid of grey hairs and the loosening of the teeth. It was the choice of lives we had in the clear woods, and in the grave we're safe surely."

One at least of my five listeners could appreciate the verbal music of Synge's drama. And, to give them their due, I think they all could. Moreover they listened with equal attention to Socrates when he addressed his judges:- "The difficulty, my friends, is not to avoid death, but to avoid unrighteousness; for that runs faster than death. I am old and move slowly, and the slower runner has overtaken me; and my accusers are keen and quick, and the faster runner, who is unrighteousness, has overtaken them. And now I depart hence condemned by you to suffer the penalty of death. . . . If you suppose that there is no consciousness, but a sleep like the sleep of him who is undisturbed even by dreams, death will be an unspeakable gain. For if a person were to select the night in which his sleep was undisturbed even by dreams, and were to compare with this the other days and nights of his life, and then had to tell us how many days and nights in his life he had passed in the course of his life better and more pleasantly than this one, I think that any man, I will not say a private man, but even the great king will not find many such days or nights when compared with the others. Now if death be of such nature, I say that to die is gain; for eternity is then only a single night. But if death is the journey to another place . . . what would not a man give if he might converse with Orpheus and Musaeus and Hesiod and Homer? Nay, if this be true, let me die again and again. . . ."

I was perfectly aware that I had modified Thursday afternoon for the sake of a particular pupil. She was often in my thoughts. I would look for her at the beginning of each day. Though the staff could wander into breakfast in the morning almost whenever they liked, the Old Lady didn't like it if we dawdled too much. It was one of the things that cropped up perennially in our circular letter at the beginning of term; "Punctuality at breakfast would be greatly appreciated." The politely-worded hint generally produced little effect. When I came at twenty-past eight or thereabouts, often the first thing my eyes did was to range quickly round the various tables to see if she was still there. The children were free to get up and go when they had finished. Often she had gone. But when she was still present a brief glimpse of that round brow with its brown hair drawn back and held in place by the narrow, black, velvet ribbon as though by a comb, reassured me. I would look across at her for less than a second and then look quickly away. It was as though the day were beginning with an undeserved and only half-expected blessing.

I had admired a number of my pupils before now; the petal-cheeked Daphne; the gentle Diana Gregg; laughing Eileen Penn; Jill Pullin with her high cheek bones, expressive mouth and shining black eyes; the grave-profiled, violet-eyed, tiny Helen Tasker; little Anne Hickson with her wealth of fairy-tale gold hair. You might say that these were an accidental bounty in the course of my work, like an unexpected white hawthorn in a laneway. And I was duly grateful for them. But that is different from allowing one's gaze to range a room quickly in search not so much of a face as of a particular person. "Is she there? Am I going to see her amongst the lingerers at one or other of the several tables?" And if she was there, I was instantly and imperceptibly heartened by the mere evidence of her continued existence.

She was the first pupil who had ever raised her eyes to mine in such a way as to make me wonder whether my own were not making a mute confession which they should not make. She was the first to make me conscious that I looked forward daily to the moment when I should see her again. I defended her in the staffroom on one occasion with such warmth that Miss Marlowe, the kindergarten mistress, wanted to know why.

It was wonderful to teach anyone as sensitive to the implications of words. Did she know that I thought it wonderful? She must have, if she had any perception at all. She may even have laughed to herself at the thought, "He rejected a kiss, and he has been looking longingly at me ever since." Or she may not have noticed anything. I told myself that if she did notice something it would speedily show, because her sympathies would almost certainly as quickly turn against me. Perhaps once, at the time of the gift of the book, or when she assured her mother than I understood her better than anyone in the world, she may have cherished some kind of mild liking for me. But she soon got over it. The boot was on the other foot now.

What must she think if she apprehended my regard for her? She may have suspected it, though only in the very vaguest fashion. Our respective circumstances were sufficient to explain that. She was grateful when I appeared to understand her. What she did not know was that everything which I told her was applicable to ninety-nine per cent of persons of my own temperament. I had merely passed on to her what I had been obliged to learn from life myself. In one sense I daresay she was introspective; in another she was extraordinarily lacking in self-consciousness. Her effect on others seemed to be completely effortless and fortuitous. She did not try to please. She lacked any ambition to make herself a force in the school. And yet in some spontaneous fashion of her own she was one. I cannot believe that she was entirely unaware of her effect upon others. She must have been. But she took it in her stride. It was so easily achieved. She had merely to be herself.

In class, because she was immediately beside me at right angles to where I sat at the head of the table, I had only, as I have told you, to look up from the book to see the impression a particular passage was making upon her. And I must have done so many times. Perhaps she was able to sense my approval of her reactions to what we read. But I doubt it. I was too professionally conscious and too much on my guard to betray the secret.

On the other hand, it was no-one's business but my own what I thought when apart from her. Dramatising the situation and postulating a set of circumstances which had not arisen and would never arise, I wrote a poem – Love's Cure – which outlined very clearly what would have been bound to happen had I captured, even momentarily, her approval. Almost on principle I occasionally snubbed her in class, just as I had been accustomed to snub the lovely Daphne. But, supposing she cared for me, such snubbings would mean little or nothing to her. I would be defeated not by them, but by one of those paradoxes which human nature furnishes to kill any vanity latent in us and to break our assurance. This was the hypothetical contingency which gave my little poem its theme; a devised situation followed by an imaginary denouement.

Love's Cure

I was loved, each day I knew
Thought more kindly to me grew,
Till at last the soul betrays
Its trembling secret in its gaze.

Ah what tenderness was there,
What unconcealed and lovely fire!
All her lips dared not decree,
Her upraised eyes said silently.

I turned aside, I gave the lie
To the least breath, to the least sigh;
Then one day, amazed, she saw
A look less carefree than before.

In that instant all was changed.
Her heart as quick against me ranged.
Now, heart-whole, she can despise
The speechless homage in my eyes.

In those first two verses, the wish is of course father to the thought. My poem says what I wanted to be true but had no grounds for believing was true. An imaginary contingency had been translated into a poem. The poem was good enough to be accepted by *The Spectator*. At the time I wondered if her parents took the paper and, supposing they read it, what their reactions would be if they had known their daughter had been its inspiration.

I could write such a poem, and yet imagine that the feelings which instigated it had gone quite unobserved. Miss Marlowe's challenging query, if not actually a gibe, came very near to being one. But I was too proud, too indifferent to what others thought to be in the least shaken by it. I had answered her truthfully and with perfect candour.

It is a mistake to be over-confident. Most of us are far more transparent than we realise. We betray our emotions by a series of trifles. I can give a good example of this. The school play was successfully over and was followed by the half-term dance. This was one of the moments of complete vindication for the Old Lady. It was the fulfilment of her boast that we were really a large family. Her staff criticised her frequently, but deep down we all had enormous admiration for her. Starting from the smallest beginnings in a rented house in the town, she had ended with our fine red-brick building perched on its knoll, our farm, our fields, our horses and all the rest, never deviating from her ideal of a rational community where the various activities of body and of mind would be given their fullest scope. She was a dictator but – if you chose the right moment – quite ready to listen to the individual contentions of others. We never discussed her age, we never even speculated about it. She was the lynch-pin, even though she had decentralised many of her own activities in favour of the various members of her family, and, with a good grace, would presently allow Arthur and Mrs. Arthur to take over when the time came.

Meanwhile, she drove herself mercilessly. She had to. It was deep in her nature. People of her temperament are liable to become neurasthenic unless they are able to express themselves in continual work. Her algebra lessons were a terror to the timid. Her age was revealed by her extreme restlessness in the evenings, when she moved about the school, on her way somewhere, but never getting there because of the distractions encountered en route. Whenever one saw her in these moments of nervous exhaustion, it brought home to one how relentlessly she drove herself. Yet even in such moments she had ten times the vitality of the average individual. She was physically frail, stooped a little, needed her gold-rimmed glasses, and her eyes often looked inexpressibly weary. But there was always the impression of an impregnable reserve of courage. Her determination came out in a hundred small ways. I have seen her on a bitter March afternoon in her long leather motoring coat watching a senior girls' hockey match, and looking, in her leather cap with ear flaps, rather like an indomitable airman who has made a crash landing in Siberia but is still hoping to get his plane into the air. Hands thrust deep in the side pockets of her coat she gazed out across the muddy field at the struggles going on around a hockey ball that had once been white but was so no longer.

Her room, just beyond the little "office" where the stationery and school books were kept, was a revelation of her mode of life. It could scarcely be called a bedroom, although there was a bed in it and a wardrobe and a mirror. In the dim abyss of time papers and books from the office next door and from all over the school had flowed into it, and its determination to be a bedroom had faltered. Lots of men have bedrooms like this, but few women; a room in which there was a continual coming and going, and at night, with eventual solitude, the still unwanted activity of mind, until at three in the morning, unable to sleep, she would give up the struggle and occupy herself with *The Times* crossword.

To get back to that mid-term summer dance. She was there, and no doubt I asked her for a waltz and we made a single dignified circuit of the room. She must have been in her late seventies, though one never thought of her in terms of age. I don't believe the children even did. In her girlhood she had met a whiskered school-inspector, on holiday in Switzerland, by name Mathew Arnold, and had walked through the streets of London to take a message from her father to William Morris. But neither these nor any other recorded facts could date her. Her personality lay outside time.

It was a very different matter when the moment came for my one dance with Anne. No customary dignified circuit of the room, quickly terminated; instead there was a counting of the precious moments and a hope that Le Poidevin would forget to stop playing. And when it ended, all too soon, I took my partner across to one of the rows of dining-room chairs ranged round the room and we chatted amicably while we waited for the music to strike up again. Le Poidevin, the music master, came from Guernsey. He was a serious musician, but on these occasions he unbent and was willing to play anything that was popular with his clientele. From time to time a ripple of good-natured amusement passed across his face, disturbing the calm of his rather prim mouth with its pursed underlip, and he seemed about to giggle.

After some particularly fine display of musical fireworks from Miss Whit, he might even break into a laugh. His intervals were long, and while they lasted his tall figure remained at the piano stool and he sank into a kind of coma. I did not mind. Now that our dance was over, the longer he remained comatose the better. Anne began to scoff a little at the kind of tunes he was giving us, too many old favourites, and far too much deliberate thumping. "Don't be blasé," I told her. "I'm not blasé. You haven't to dance, like I have, with some of the smaller boys. If they ask you, you can't very well refuse. They tread on your feet the whole time, and that would put you in a bad humour even with good music."

Periodically in response to public demand, we were given a "Paul Jones". An outer and inner circle were formed to revolve in opposite directions. As they did so, the boys dragged furiously ahead or hung back in their efforts to avoid certain unwanted partners. Quite early in the evening, in the course of the first Paul Jones, I found myself opposite Anne when the music stopped. We danced together and when, in the course of a similar circulation later, it looked as though precisely the same good fortune might befall me, I stiffened abruptly and rigidly lest I should be carried one step further, so that it must almost certainly have been noticeable to the housekeeper, Miss Tanner, who was next in the inner circle, and who would have been my partner if Le Poidevin had continued playing a moment longer.

An episode like this is a straw that shows which way the wind is blowing. And there were other similar ones. I have a most vivid recollection of an incident which occurred not long afterwards. I had promised her another book, an anthology which contained several contributions by me, and she came down next morning accompanied by a friend to the bungalow to get it. I unearthed the volume in my room and went out along the garden path to meet her, saying, "I spoil you, you know. Everyone does." "Write my name in it, please." "Of course." She thanked me and a curious twisted expression came into her face, which might mean tears or anything. Of all my pupils she lived most in her emotions. Her contemporaries had either none to speak of or they kept them in stricter control and never betrayed them. I went back into the bungalow on that occasion with a curious sense of relief. By merely telling her that I spoiled her, I had made a confession which I never dreamed I would have the courage to make. In

Donegal, in the course of the holidays, I got a letter from her, and for a whole day thought only of the pleasure of answering it.

I am wasting my time telling you all this, for you are bound to misunderstand me. Our gradations of feeling towards another person cannot be put into words. We ourselves are unaware of the different stages. The man in the street is inarticulate. He may say to you, "I was crazy about her," or, "What she did to me I don't know." But that is the furthest he will ever get to a confession, if he can bring himself even to say as much. A writer is different. He is aware of his predicament. One part of him wants to leave on record exactly what happened; another part wants to understand it. I am not talking of those who write for entertainment or for their livelihood, or for both these objectives; people in search not of truth but of verisimilitude. Serious novelists of course hope to make some contribution to the greater understanding of human nature. They are the giants of their profession and their insight is matched by their powers of invention. I am interested merely in investigating our human mystery. And I find it easiest to study it in myself. Not that it gets me very far. I welcome emotion and I respect intelligence, and try to draw my deductions with the aid of these two. I am not a Catholic, but I was highly flattered when a man who was at one time head of the Jesuit Order in England and the possessor of a brilliant mind wrote to me that he had found in my poems "a wisdom which is centred on the deep intimations and lessons of love." And he added, "You do express the heart." What higher praise could one want, even if the heart in our time has ceased to be what it once was, the physical metaphor for love? An unsatisfactory symbol, you may say? Why then is that organ known to beat faster merely on the most slender provocation from some entirely psychological stimulus?

One can only express the heart if one understands a little of its method of functioning. I doubt if I do. I am making you my consultant. All you have to do is to listen to a few recorded symptoms from a medical case-book. You can form your own conclusions. You may even shake your head knowingly at some of the things I tell you. What you must not imagine is that I took everything which I am describing to you with very great serious-ness at the time. It was just something incidental which was best kept to myself. It added a certain anxious and yet pleasurable tension to life. I did not question it. I did not theorise about it. I know that my disposition inclines to sentiment; but not to sentimentality. That is a bogus by-product of self-indulgent egoism. I was certainly not proud of what was happening to me; neither was I ashamed. I knew what had happened; and I made no attempt to rationalise it. If I had done so, it would have been merely to discover its absurdity.

I have always found it hard to envisage Divine Love, although people talk so glibly about it. But suppose there is a Being capable of discovering in every apparently commonplace individual certain traits, potentialities, aspirations capable of arousing a degree of Divine interest and compassion comparable to the goodwill that the lover feels towards the beloved – that indeed would be god-like. It would be goodwill and understanding in depth. Fortunate indeed are those capable of inspiring such a reaction in a fellow human-being. The rest must just be content to wait and hope that God will demonstrate His love for them. My feelings towards Anne at the deepest level were disinterested; partly a recognition that here was a personality of a different order – quite different, for I could see its effect on others. Like a chord struck on a piano, or like those few notes in a Chopin prelude where every intervening moment of silence seems even more eloquent than the preceding or subsequent sounds from the keyboard, she registered in my consciousness.

I was clear about my attitude to her. But I am not clear, and have never been clear, about her attitude to me. In saner moments, I decided that her proffer of a kiss after the gift of the book was simply the natural and expected reaction of an impulsive adolescent, and that I had taken it too seriously. The pedagogue in me had come out of the episode with flying colours, smug idiot that he was. It occurs to me now however, that I may have had my own subconscious reasons for over-stressing my disinterested behaviour on that occasion. It gave oblique reassurance. If the kiss was merely the spontaneous gesture of youth, there would have been no need to reject it. My taking the whole episode so seriously implied I held some place in her regard.

Nevertheless, my reaction at the time had been as spontaneous as hers. It was in accordance with every acceptable tradition in my profession. Had I a secret and unrealised motive for uprating the repulsed kiss? There was at least this justification for my smugness – it would have seemed very wonderful indeed to be kissed by her; for kisses on the stockmarket quotation of my emotions have so high a rating that there is practically no business ever done in them. It had been flattering to be told by her mother that I understood her "better than anyone in the world", though the same could be said of a helpful psychologist or of a sympathetic local vicar. But to have won her affection as an individual, to have ceased to be one of those lay figures – they are little more than that – which the staff of a school represent to those whom they teach – that would have been something worth having.

I may be wronging myself in this exhaustive psychological dissection. For the strange thing is that I have seldom consciously wanted to be loved by anyone. It would mean an invasion of my privacy; it might even be an actual embarrassment. Lurking in me has always been that curious *Noli me tangere*, a dread that any living creature should experience for me the kind of idealised affection which I am capable of feeling for them. All I have ever asked is permission to love and admire.

As for Anne, she probably thought of both Underwood and myself as beings belonging to another world, shadowy Titans. It would never occur to her that she could exercise anything but the mildest fascination over either of us. Boys were different. There she may have been aware of their vulnerability and her own power. Actually she appeared to pay them little attention. Her home influences were very much on the side of the world of the imagination. I got the impression of a Wordsworthian innocence, and of a poetry-nurtured childhood which was far removed from all earthiness. Her assurance, her crystal-clear voice with its sardonic inflexions, her apparent precocity were all misleading. Behind this effective facade, behind the schoolgirl heartlessness which left David Nicoll's letters unanswered, lay a nature fundamentally inexperienced, all its values taken from poets long dead.

I was, as I have told you, a long way removed from being sentimental about the lady, if by sentiment is meant that mawkish self-indulgent pre-occupation which longs for acceptance, for recognition of some kind. I expected nothing. I desired nothing, beyond being allowed to possess a harmless and quite innocent secret of my own.

Indeed it gave me satisfaction to think that my behaviour towards her differed – I am speaking of outward behaviour, not my attitude of mind – in no degree from that towards any of my other pupils. I was even glad when given a chance to show this. One day Joan Wilson consulted me about some matter of discipline amongst the boys, important enough to have worried her but not important enough for me to remember what it was now. I respected her for having had the integrity to worry about the matter, and, after thinking it over, I decided that it was not something for me to deal with and that I had better refer the whole thing to Arthur. I did so, but only after first obtaining permission from Joan.

I reported the affair and action was duly taken.

When I went into the library the following morning, Anne was kneeling beside her book locker and, looking up, she accused me of betraying a confidence.

"Mind your own jolly business. It has absolutely nothing to do with you," I snapped at her in front of the others.

It was a relief to be angry with her – salt rubbed into the secret wound of sentiment. It restored the balance. It convinced me that she was just one among many, and re-established me in my own eyes as a master who was not afraid to flatten his favourite pupil.

Later that day, however, it dawned on me that it was at least possible that my feelings were in danger of becoming obvious to the staff. I observed them closely for a few days. They showed no sign. The Hickson family were a different matter. They were all so busy that it was highly unlikely they would ever notice the reactions of a member of their staff to a particular pupil. On the other hand, Miss Whit had been in the school so long and was so much in the confidence of the Old Lady that she would almost certainly have drawn attention to the situation had she felt it necessary. But no-one in the whole school, except Miss Marlowe, with her scornful "Why are you always defending her?", had dropped even a faint hint that they were aware of anything.

When the latter asked her question, "Why are you always sticking up for her?" I replied, "Because of all my pupils she is the one who best understands poetry." A little more courage and I might have added, "And probably love. The two go together." A little more malice on her side and she would have said, "We all pity you at staff meetings when her name comes up. In your case, you should be allowed to contribute your verdict upon her on paper like the matrons do." The matrons did not attend staff supper. They were otherwise occupied, seeing the various dormitories to bed. And so they were asked to express their opinion on selected individuals in this way and the Old Lady had their lists in front of her on the table.

I had come to Anne's defence on more than one occasion. I imagined that I was disinterested. But no-one is disinterested who hungers for an occasional glimpse of a particular face. It would have shocked me if my colleagues had thought that I was behaving unprofessionally. That would have been an indictment of my whole integrity as a teacher; and as a man. It was a different matter if, as was possible, they had agreed to discreetly overlook my subjugation. But supposing one of them, in a moment of irritation, had begun asking awkward questions and had launched a frontal attack? "Why is it she who always takes any shoeless horse to the forge? What's this about lessons round the fire on Thursday afternoon? You think you've sweated it out of your system. You think she's just a pupil like any other pupil. You say she's leaving before long and you may never see her again. Listen, my friend, you imagine you are telling the truth. But you are not. You are in love with Anne, and you will always be in love with her, in some measure, till the end of time. She's going away and, as you say, you may never see her again. But you will always be in love with the immeasurable. People are what you want them to be. What you love most of all is the idea of the person which you carry within yourself. You enjoy reading poetry. But that's not enough. You are convinced that one ought to live poetry too. And so you go through life looking everywhere for the living poem. Childhood pleases you because it is fresh from the mint. The coin has not yet been rubbed and defaced. You can find redeeming features in all your pupils simply because they are young and hopeful. And you like Anne because she is the nearest thing to a living poem in this whole school."

A damning indictment had someone ever chosen to make it. And in a sense it was all true. But in another sense it was completely false. For if our affections are as subjective, as self-created a matter as this, why should they turn towards any particular object in preference to any other? The whole alphabet is there to chose from. Why not L, M, N, or O? If I had elected for the letter A, it must be because for me it held some special quality. Other pupils had revealed charm, grace, beauty; their intelligence had outstripped hers; they were as vital, more vital in certain re-

spects. I liked them and approved them. But they did not touch me
in any personal way. They were just part of the general poetry of
life. But Anne was herself a poem. She was a reminder of one of
the most important verities of existence. My interest in her, my
reverence for her, was an awakening of that reverence which one
should perhaps feel for the hidden potential in every individual.

I was not certain by any means that I was doing her a service in
taking a special interest in her. There was an ambiguity even in
that bracing, disinterested note which I brought to her difficulties. Because, no matter how bracing it might be, there was always
an unspoken postscript to it, "I urge you to do this or to be that.
But it must be fairly plain to you that I urge it because I like you in
a very special degree."

This implicit postscript could devalue all that had gone before.
It was not to her advantage to be at the mercy of her moods no
matter how much I may have tried to arm her against them or
how perceptive I may have aided her to make her attitude to these
to be. Had I really done her a disservice by helping her to cultivate
her sensibility? Was sensitivity her enemy rather than her friend
and should I have been at some pains to immunise her against it?

From time to time I tried to do so. I presented the facade of a
brusque extrovert. But it is doubtful if she was taken in by it. Her
own instictive defence had always been an assumed hardness, a
kind of surface cynicism. But it was a poor one, an attempt to solve
the problem by denying its existence. If I understood her – and I
was convinced that I did – it was simply because I understood
myself. We were in the same boat, at the mercy of every poignant
impression, But I was adult. I could contemplate the future
curtailment of sensibility with a feeling of faint relief. I could even
write – in anticipation of such a time – a poem entitled
Resignation:-

So after all it seems
If time and fate and care
Choose to conspire together
With the heart's wear and tear,
With the indwelling fear
And the indwelling flaw
A day might come when hope
Would throb no more?

If such a day should come,
Tell me, might one then find
The foe that seemed so dread
Gentle-eyed grown and kind?
Might one, without condition
Or clause, be glad to lay
On the broad bosom of death
Even hope away?

It is almost certain that I was more transparent in my attitude to
her than I liked to admit. I have spoken of the boredom of the
Sunday evening conversazione in the Old Lady's drawing-room.
The Friday fortnightly staff-meeting at supper in the Raphael
was a more interesting but in many ways a more formidable
occasion. At five-to-seven we would assemble in that class-room in
front of the red brick fireplace which, if it was winter, would have
a blazing log fire in the high grate. The long, oval table, laid for
supper, awaited its guests and the staff would gather for the meal,
slowly, one by one. Miss Arnold would leave her studio-cum-
residence and make her way up the front avenue, since the
short-cut through the rock-garden was too steep and uncertain
for someone lame and dependent upon a stick. Passing through
the tiny projecting porch, which smelt of poodle and of leather
overcoats and riding whips, she would remove her wraps as she
stood by the great oak-dresser in the front hall with its shelves of
blue china plates and its broad ledge on which letters for the staff
were laid out. In winter this would mean divesting herself of a
number of anonymous garments suggestive of an arctic explorer
rather than of an elderly art and elocution mistress. But if it was
late spring she would have discarded the Balaclava helmet,
although there was still the shawl. Having shed it, she would limp
through the big well-lit dining-hall to reach the Raphael by the
nearer of its two doors.

Upstairs in the staff-room we had been exhorting one another
not to prolong the debate.

"Don't worry about the laziness or the stupidity or the irrespon-
sibilities of those who always hold us up. Give them any card you
like, but don't keep us there all night."

The irony of "the cards", which were then allotted by us, but
which would not be distributed until assembly in the gymnasium
on Saturday morning, was that they had a terminology of their

own which was quite different from the generally-accepted one. The vast majority were blue, and had a space for an agreed assessment of the previous fortnight's record for each pupil. They assessed both Conduct and Diligence. If the staff concurred in giving anyone "double E" – and there were quite a number of such agreements – it meant that the recipient was more or less impeccable in both respects. But linguistic devaluation followed hard on this orthodox beginning. "Good' for Conduct was not really such high praise; it only meant moderate. And "Fair" for Diligence would have been better expressed by "Pretty Ghastly". "Poor" implied absolute condemnation. And a white card, instead of the customary blue, so far from being the token of a blameless life, was actually an indication that the offender was almost on the verge of expulsion. Only a really grave misdemeanour ensured one, and its award created a mild sensation at the supper table; still more when it was handed to the child by the Old Lady next day.

The hazards of a Friday staff-meeting were immense. The discussion did not begin until one had been fortified by the first course of the meal. One almost held one's breath until certain highly debatable names were safely past. "Allah be praised! they're going to let So-and-so have his 'double E'." And then a voice would pipe up, "No, he can't possibly have it for work. He hasn't done a tap for me this week." Twenty minutes later the merits or demerits of the individual in question would still be under discussion. A kind of paralysis had taken over, and we would seem incapable of passing on to the next name on the list. I always dreaded prolonged staff-meetings, although my colleagues regarded me as one of the worst offenders when it came to climbing onto a hobby horse and so delaying the proceedings.

But now Friday evening began to hold another and personal terror for me. During all its earlier stages, I lived in a kind of mild nightmare. I dreaded the moment when Anne's name would come up and I might betray by some minute reaction the special interest I took in her. Since we began at the bottom of the school with the youngest children, my anxiety lasted for almost the whole evening. When we reached her, and her name after endless delay was at last called, would I flinch? Would I suddenly redden, and would the whole table see that I was embarrassed? thus confirming certain already existent suspicions? The nearer we drew to the top form the more anxious I became to have a piece of bread which I could assiduously crumble, the more earnest and intent became my discussion of the names immediately before hers so that there would be a greater excuse for saying little or nothing when she was reached. The moment came, and I would stiffen slightly in a way that I hoped no-one could possibly notice. By then, I had pulled myself together with a kind of defiant self-scorn, as though shouting to the whole table:"Look at me! Yes, look at me! Look as closely as you like but you will see nothing! My *sang froid* is complete. Not by the flicker of an eyelid have I indicated that the subject of our present debate is of any greater interest to me than the merits and demerits of that inky little ruffian on whom we were wasting our time half an hour ago."

It was an ordeal I had come to expect. I had the feeling sometimes that my colleagues were expecting it too. Some of them might be already thinking: "Now he's for it! How will he manage this week?" Feeling that I was losing my cool, I might as a last resort raise some issue which directly concerned her, and discuss, critically and impersonally, whether she should take the second English paper or not in the school certificate as though this were a point of grave academic interest to me. Even when her card was quickly decided, my troubles were not over, for if it had been a problem to conceal my anxiety before her name was mentioned, it became an equally grave one to conceal my relief once it has been safely dismissed.

I know what you are going to ask and have been waiting to ask for the last half hour. What did my wife think of all this? Was she completely unaware of it? Was I such a consummate actor that it all passed unnoticed by her?

No, of course she was aware of it. But in a happy marriage – and ours was a happy one despite the violence of its explosive moments – each partner always regards, or comes gradually to regard, magnanimity as an essential element in mutual love. It would have seemed to us undignified to create a scene. Rational spirits concede to one another the right to admire or to be admired, even though to be a witness of such admiration may give rise to a certain amount of thoughtful reflection and even distress. A mixture of pride, generosity and understanding prevented us – since no treachery was ever involved – from indulging in anything so mean-spirited as jealousy.

A cynic may question all this. But he would be wrong. If I had not been in love with my wife and altogether happy in the physical expression of our love; if we had not had many ideals in common and shared an ambition to do the best by our children, there might be some excuse for theorising on different lines and saying that what prompted me on this occasion was merely a sublimated variety of that desire, shared by countless thousands, to escape from some unacceptable physical tie into an imagined promised land. But in our marriage, we were welded together not merely by shared principles but by a strong and genuine mutual acceptability. We regarded marriage as an art rather than a science, and an art which exacted patient and intelligent apprenticeship.

Where I was concerned, Anne was a complete irrelevance in any even remotely sexual respect. And the same was axiomatic when it came to defining her attitude to me. She probably knew that I admired her. But things were different in those days. It would have seemed inconceivable to her that anyone in my position should love a schoolgirl, and indeed almost as inconceivable that unattached adults, as far removed from her in age as Underwood and my brother-in-law, when she presently met him, should regard her as anything except a gangling adolescent at – to use her own expression – "this dreadful age".

"And, for yourself, what did you wish?"

I have explained that several times already. Merely the pleasure of being in her company; of sharing a few of her thoughts; of, in some way or other, influencing her future favourably.

My wife was invariably present at the Friday meeting, and I never doubted that she frequently sensed what was happening in my mind. Wives are perceptive. Mine could walk into a room and know instantly if there was any new face there which was likely to meet with my approval. Almost invariably she shared this approval. And she realised that – certainly for some couples – love is less threatened by a straying eye or a romantic disposition than it is by the iron fetters of an enforced devotion. It was not a crime in her eyes to recognise beauty or charm; and she would have felt sorry for any wife whose husband was completely incapable of such recognition, for it would come dangerously near to an admission that such apathy might very easily accompany lack of appreciation of her.

Where she showed her magnanimity most of all, I think, was in her silence, her refusal to offer any comment whatever upon what she knew was a private business of the heart. This was all the more praiseworthy in someone who, when over-tired, could be fiery about mere trifles. It revealed the nobility of her nature. She saw many faults in me, but she did not count my susceptibility as one of them. A sense of reverence for personal emotion sealed our lips when it came to any occasion of deeper feeling. Neither of us would ever have dreamed of yielding to curiosity, much less of indulging in the vulgarity of abuse.

She never commented to me upon what was happening. But some years later she told me that Underwood, who was the close friend of both of us, had discussed it with her. He may have broached the subject because he imagined the situation held its dangers. What is made probable from this disclosure is that everyone knew. Indeed, I have almost positive proof that this was so. Years later, meeting at a sherry party someone who had been gym mistress at the school for part of the time when we were there, I said to her,

"Some day I think I'll write a book about that school. There was so much about it which was utterly distinctive. If I do write it, I know what I shall call it – The Pupil."

And then, in a moment of puckish daring, and, looking her straight in the eyes, I asked, challengingly,

"Who was the pupil?"

Without a moment's hesitation, she gave the correct name. After nearly two decades, it came instantly to her lips. Here was proof positive how vain my efforts at dissimulation on Friday evenings had been.

I had had my answer and I did not pursue the topic further; not even to confirm to her the accuracy of her reply. I suppose all that I have been telling you occupied a year and a half, or perhaps two years, of my twelve at Swanage, and you must not over-estimate its importance. It stands out simply because any lyrical element in our lives is red-lettered in memory as though we really belonged to a different, and in one sense, a more real world, like a foreigner in a great city who hears his tongue spoken for the first time for many months by a passing stranger, so all such occasions are endowed with powers of survival for us.

The cloud of war was just beginning to gather over Europe

once more, a cloud no larger than a man's hand. And as you know
from your Old Testament, thunder and torrential rain – in this
case far from providential – can be the sequels to such a slight
token. I liked my work, I liked my teaching, I liked my mental
possession of all that green countryside on horseback with the
children. It will give you an idea of my contentment with my lot
when I tell you that I envisaged ending my days there. I even
secured a forty-year lease on my bungalow. Why? Because I was living a civilised life in delightful surroundings. Countless objectives
were being pursued all around me: scouts, guides, farming and
gardening classes, auditions for the Poetry Society, drawing and
painting examinations, and all the rest. The Old Lady herself was
tireless, though often she looked tired. One would see wisps of
grey hair playing around her forehead as she came along the
passage, holding a bunch of books which did not include the one
she wanted; distressed by the loss of her mark-book, but inflexibly
determined to run it to earth. She had my full sympathy. I was
always losing mine. In the gym corridor her voice might ring out
authoritatively, "Arthur!" It was the voice of an autocrat. On
these occasions I would ask myself did I idealise her and was she
really Mother Spider in whose web all the members of her family
were caught? Certainly not her elder daughter, who adored her,
and whose shield and defender she was on all occasions. Jo could
be petulant; she could lose her temper completely with a French
class and make herself ridiculous. It was her mother's gladly-
accepted role to pour oil on such troubled waters. There was a
bond of deep affection between the two. Jo had great artistic
talent and could always depend on the Old Lady for approval of
her latest water-colour. She was clever with her hands. She did
wonderful leatherwork. When she really wished to show her skill,
she showed it in a pair of fur gloves for her mother. They were
united in their defence of Pierrot, the most loathsome poodle on
earth. He was cordially detested by all the staff because of his
habit of lying under classroom tables, unseen, but very quickly
noted by every nostril in the class, for he smelt like half a barrel of
dead fish. Pierrot was not as moribund as this might seem to
indicate. He would accompany the horses on some of our longest
rides and had recently fathered a litter of young poodles which Jo
was bringing up. His dynasty appeared secured. So dear was he to
his mistress that she had even edited his autobiography for the

school magazine. Though the daughter had tended lately to transfer her affection to Pierrot's progeny, the Old Lady herself was steadfast in her loyalty to her old and very smelly friend. Breeding poodles and keeshunds was only one aspect of family versatility. Jo played the cello. Arthur had half-a-dozen hobbies. Pip was best at teaching, but could turn her hand to most things. She was the owner of Crusoe, the huge Irish wolf-hound who came on rides with us. Vera had her Angora rabbits. All this was seen as part of a full existence. Everything was woven into the texture of the community. Horses, dogs, the farm, pets, newts in an aquarium, and the rest, helped to make up a full life, and so a school must have them. Not that the family were either doggy or horsey to any special degree.

Thanks to my post-war farming course in Jersey, I was a little more in sympathy with such activities than were my colleagues. Indignant voices were raised from time to time in the staffroom. "Have you heard the latest? Mansfield was taking a gardening class down by Miss Arnold's studio and one of the boys drove a fork through his own foot." "Silly young ass!" "He was wearing gumboots!" "Even so he ought to be able to see his own foot." "Why do they do all these things? They weren't sent to school to learn gardening. I could do with that period for my history. Small girls in blue jeans pouring pig-swill into a trough may look wonderful in the school prospectus, but does it really matter that much?"

It is true I had my own grumbles: Sunday evening discussions on the League of Nations and the like. The pace of life was too hot. One was surprised the children did not flag under it. The Old Lady was instantly uneasy if she thought that any child might be at the Devil's mercy through lack of occupation. It had become an obsession with her. But I had won my battle over the rest period. Every three weeks my EMG handmade gramophone was brought up to the school. It might look antediluvian, though both Delius and Paul Robeson were glad to own one. I enjoyed my role as impresario, introducing the recumbent figures swathed in their rugs on the gym floor, to a Spanish Jota of de Falla, or to the death of Don Quixote sung – with sobs from Sancho, for he doubled the two roles when recording it – by Chaliapin.

This, like the Sunday evening concerts and readings, was only one of the many touches which made school life not school life at

all but a cultured oasis in a world that – if you were reading the
newspapers – seemed to be heading resolutely towards barbar-
ism. One could go into the gym after supper and chance on a
folk-dancing class and remain for a minute or two to watch the
first couple; backs very straight, arms hanging loosely by the sides,
fingers extended, one dancer in a bright blue gingham frock
which suited her square-cut freckled face, the other gentle-
expressioned and charming, in a flowered muslin dress with a
narrow, round, white collar and two coloured streamer ribbons
tied in a little bow at her throat. The dance was all verve, spon-
taneity and bravura, a mixture of ease and rigidity, loosely-
swinging arms, upright heads, and shoulders thrown back.

Of course I enjoyed such moments, just as I enjoyed the tea-
parties prepared down at our own bungalow for the voracious
appetites of certain especially gallant youths who had distinguished themselves recently in a rugger match; or for the tennis
six, which my wife coached and which brought off victories over
various neighbouring schools in summer. And, as well as these
group invitations, we liked to have three or four individuals down
from time to time, and even entertained one eight-year-old for a
whole term whose parents had lost all their money in a business
crash and could no longer afford her boarding-fees. All contacts
on these lines were a reminder that I was not rowing dispiritedly
chained to my oar in some pedagogic galley. I was a free citizen in
a free community, engaged in finding out how much life has to
offer the innocent and the intelligent. And – believe it or not – it
was in just the same spirit that I congratulated myself on having a
pupil to whom poetry meant everything and whose response to
literature, compared to the average response, differed almost as
much as the tone of a superb violin differs from the instrument of
a street-fiddler.

I was not to have her much longer. She was taking her departure at the end of the term. She would sit for school certificate in
July but whether she obtained it or not made no difference. She
would not be returning to us. It had been decided that it was time
for her to devote all her energies to music.

Her approaching departure left me with a feeling of mild resentment, not against her parents for reaching this decision, but
against circumstance. It seemed too early for her to give up the
advantages of community life; that is, if they had ever meant

anything to her. Had the school influenced her at all? Behind all the educational props, agricultural, horticultural, harmonic, literary, equestrian, lay ultimately, I suppose, the deep, Quaker conviction that character is everything, and that everything without character is nothing. Perhaps they flattered themselves in their assumption that they were creating character. Many of their pupils might be found today willing to declare, "The school did not influence me in the smallest degree. I was what I became before I ever arrived there and I laugh to scorn your fantastic – your pathetic – notion that you were shaping and moulding me. All we got was by shrewd observation of a few adult characteristics, passed on to us, obliquely, by persons who themselves had learnt something from life."

Anne might well have said the same. But I would prefer to believe that the school did exercise a modicum of influence, although what that influence was it would have been hard to define, except that it lay always on the side of a free flowering of personality. Thereto I contributed in some small degree. The Indian sage, Patanjali, affirmed that "the universe exists for purposes of soul." And, in the same way, on a much smaller scale, I used to feel, "This school exists for purposes of soul."

It was for Anne's sake, or rather, as I told myself at the time, "for purposes of soul", that I founded the poetry society. I had first promised to found one when she had complained that the school cared nothing for poetry. After endless delays, the promise was fulfilled. The exact details of its membership are very vague in my memory. Whereas I could name you a dozen or more guests who came to our Saturday afternoon parties down at the bungalow, I cannot single out any other members of that poetry society except two who came from outside the school. These two, Hilda and Mary Spencer-Watson, together with my wife and Anne, made up the sum total of its membership, or so it seems to me now.

We were all five of us poetry-lovers, all with a certain capacity for reading aloud. My wife reads a poem with an almost instinctive consideration for its content and music, so that it seems to acquire a living and audible personality of its own. You recall it as you recall the beauty or distinction of a human face. According to A.E., poets are the soul of a nation. I would modify this and say that they are here to reveal the human soul to itself.

We read in the garden of our bungalow. On at least one occasion Anne and her mother came, and we read on the grass in front of Dunshay Manor as guests of the Spencer-Watsons. Spencer-Watson himself was dead. He had been an artist and a great painter of horses. On more than one occasion Hilda, and Mary as a small child, had figured on their mounts on the downs in the annual exhibition of the Royal Academy. Now they still rode; but there was no-one to paint them. Hilda was Australian by birth, wealthy, it was said, in her own right, and one of those rare individuals to whom one can find absolutely no parallel in all one's acquaintance. Tall, cadaverous, a female Don Quixote without armour, wearing, instead of a helmet, a wide, brightly-coloured Mexican straw hat, and driving occasionally into Swanage in a low dog-cart, drawn by two white mules and with two spotted Dalmatians running beneath it, their noses almost touching the axle-rod. Face narrow, nose long, chin pronounced, she was nevertheless as handsome a woman as one could see; but in a mode different from everyone else. Voice mannered, incisive yet persuasive; jet black hair divided down the centre and drawn flat over each brow. Sitting behind her once at the school play, I detected a narrow line of snow-white either side of the division. It surprised me and I kept the secret even from my wife. For Hilda was indefatigable, in her daily life and in her devotion to her art which was mime. She kept Arab horses, a small Jersey herd, and a bull which was unchivalrous enough to break her leg on one occasion while being led out to pasture. In the fields behind their secluded Elizabethan manor house, hidden in a cleft half-a-mile back from the Corfe Road, one could feel completely safe from the intrusions of the world. A notice on the wooden gate of the short straggling avenue asked the prospective caller to telephone before going any further. Not even Hilda's closest friends were allowed a casual visit. Her reactions were those of Malvolio, "Go off; I discard you: Let me enjoy my private."

The relationship between mother and daughter was a remarkable one. It was possible to see Hilda as an exacting, iron-willed monomaniac, battening on the saintly devotion of her daughter and sacrificing even the latter's youth and talent as a sculptress to her own single pre-occupation with what some regarded as little more than an excuse for exhibitionism. Mary was a lovely creature, with a flower-like, slightly Russian type of beauty; graceful;

well but strongly built; a perfect foil to the dramatic angularity of her tall mother. She was generally the female principle in their mimes, in contrast to her mother's freakish, quixotic masculinity, but I have seen her dance a male part in a mime on war with vigorous and striking effect.

Her dancing was excellent; quite as significant, often even more significant than Hilda's. Yet to those who knew the circumstances of her life her collaboration seemed sometimes to be prompted by an ulterior motive. Like everything else, it was done to make her mother happy. For Mary in many ways was a saint. Hilda lived upon her own nerves. Mary, with endless patience, put up with her pernickety precision over trifles – "Darling, don't you think we could sometimes have the Jensen silver spoon with the honey and not this hideous thing?"; "Darling, are you ever going to remember that we decided not to hang the Paraguayan gourd there any longer?" This preoccupation with domestic triviality went on all the time. Mary accepted it, even in front of strangers, patiently and with a tolerant smile. There was an almost masculine tenderness in the way in which she put up with her mother's oblique grumbles and brushed them good-humouredly aside. She enjoyed their periodic performances in the tiny thatched mime-theatre which stood above the great pond and to one side of the very low stone enclosure which was the manor's final defence, and she accepted the homage offered her after their shows with a kind of countrified modesty that suggested Jeanne d'Arc: her eyes lit up with almost a twinkle, and across her wide, beautiful and mobile mouth would flash a sudden smile, revealing her very even white teeth. But you realised that what pleased Mary most of all was the thought that her mother, now, after weeks of preparation, was for a few instants content and filled with a sense of achievement. No doubt she felt herself more necessary than ever since her artist-father's death. Hilda's incessant fixation with trivia was a minor irrelevance. Mary pretended not to notice it. What a costly thing real love of any kind is! There is something a little frightening about it. Mary's whole life was knit inextricably to that of her mother and to the lovely old manorhouse and the daily round of quite hard work with cattle and horses. If sour old Carlyle were depicting the situation, I can see him presenting Hilda as a prancing, jigging, feather-witted, tyrannical egoist, intent only on her own periodic posturings.

And it would be true in one sense; and hideously false in another. She was a dedicated servant of her art, a complete muddle-head about anything as complicated as politics or philosophy, but one of those very few persons who make you feel that intellect is not really necessary, provided one is bountifully endowed with artistic intuition.

When I met them first and was lucky enough to be invited to their performances, I got the impression that theirs was the perfect collaboration. Mary had been her pupil since she was three. Years later she would tell me that everything which was creative in their performances came from her mother. She herself was only the obedient – and incidentally the very talented – interpretess of her mother's ideas. As well might Fonteyn claim to have had a hand in the invention of Giselle in the first instance as for her to make any claim to have had a hand in the origination of a particular mime.

I begin to believe now that this may well have been the case. A streak of genius in Hilda prompted her, as I suppose it prompts the vast majority of persons of genius, to be guided by her intuitions rather than by any logical system or doctrinaire theories. Buried deep in her subconscious, she no doubt had many of the submerged theories of the artist, but she could not have voiced them, nor I believe would she have wished to voice them. If she worked on any system it was simply that of trial and error. And in Mary – as in herself – she had developed a perfect instrument to achieve her varied objectives. No doubt any ballet-mistress does something of the sort. But the ballet-mistress is following a rule of thumb. She is teaching something that has been taught for generations. Hilda's aim went much further than that and was truly that of the inspired choreographer. She wanted to create, to create the visual poetry of appropriate gesture. She wanted to supplement music by making it as it were bilingual. In the title of a mime, she might give a hint of what her intention was, but she left it to you – it would have been quite impossible for her to have taken the initiative in the matter – to understand what it was that she was saying to you. What she offered was beauty, and, as we all know, beauty lies beyond definition and must be its own interpreter. On the other hand, in the language of gesture, she was capable of demonstrating to her partner exactly what she wanted and her partner must have had a remarkable instinctive gift for quickly picking up the directive and manifesting the inner significance of the mime in a way that was not merely adequate but entirely beautiful.

It was only after I had known them both for a number of years, and after Hilda had had to endure the irritation of a long and painful recovery from the violence of that inconsiderate bull, who broke her leg, that I first began, I suppose, to wonder sometimes whether the daughter was not being exploited by the mother. What may have helped to prompt the idea was the fact that Mary had developed a taste for plastic art and was revealing a considerable talent as a sculptress. I suppose I wondered whether as an artist in one line, it would be possible for her to add another, and to serve two masters. But in blaming Hilda, I was absolutely and entirely wrong. She encouraged the development of the new talent from the very start and would eventually and without complaint become the solitary interpretess of her mime inspirations.

It was on the small enclosed lawn immediately in front of the low building of weathered Purbeck stone that we sat on rugs to read poetry on the one occasion that the short-lived, modestly-numbered poetry society met there. Then Anne was taken into the manor for tea and to enjoy the brightly coloured paintings, mostly of equine subjects, which lightened up the walls of its dark rooms. Of course on an occasion like this she was enjoying special privilege, though in a sense it was she herself who was responsible for it, since she was the one who had protested that the school ought to give poetry its due.

Anne was leaving, and I would miss her. All she had ever meant to me was an increased lyrical awareness of life and personality. But that, as you should know, is a lot. If there was any drama – though, as I keep insisting, there was not – now was the obvious moment for the arrival of a *deus ex machina*. And indeed one appeared, or at least a potential one, in the shape of the second of my wife's three brothers. If I had wanted someone who would scale down my interest in my pupil to a more suitable level, here was the very man. And he held a number of qualifications that put him in the picture. I had met the whole family when travelling in Sicily, and had been introduced to them in the Corso Umberto in Taormina. I am not a connoisseur in masculine good-looks, but I was immediately struck by the distinguished features of the tall, white-haired, handsome father in his black clericals, and still more by those of his eighteen-year-old son, who, placed beside the Apollo Belvedere, would have made the latter's good looks appear stereotyped and conventional. He was the handsomest young man I have ever encountered. This "stunner" – to use a slang phrase of the period – had just left Lancing and, before long, would be going up to Christ Church, where his elder brother had preceded him. He never seemed conscious of anything special in his appearance and, when he got to Oxford, he would remain unspoilt by the adulation alike of dons and of fellow-undergraduates.

"Reggie" descended on us, on leave from the Sudan where he was a civil servant. It was not his first visit, and he had always been made welcome at the school. His arrival furnished an opportunity to prove indubitably to myself that my interest in Anne was – if this is not a contradiction in terms – completely disinterested. She was almost the first person to whom I introduced him.

He could be charming to the opposite sex. But the rules of his service pledged him not to marry for five years. He was now well into his twenties and surviving his enforced bachelorhood with apparent calm, helped, it may have been, by recollections of an unattainable cousin, daughter of the governor of his province, whose parents had had other and more ambitious plans for her. He would jest about what he called his chastity-belt. But, since he had lots of men friends, was a keen yachtsman and out-of-doors man, it was not proving such a frustration. Besides, his good looks had made him highly cautious where girls were concerned, lest his friendship should be misunderstood. Like a nervous setter, he was gun-shy; partly for the reasons I have given; partly, perhaps, by disposition.

His visit began a few days before half-term which in summer, was the most social occasion of the whole year. Our festivities held out no prospect of enjoyment to him; he would have preferred to miss them. But he liked to come back to our retreat in the fields, and was the easiest of guests to entertain. He had stayed with us before, and all he wanted to do was to join in our daily life so far as our school involvements permitted. He told us about his round of duties in the distant province of Darfu. A very unpleasant experience had befallen him since his last leave. Its distressing details were disclosed to us now. He had taken an escort to a remote part of the province to bring in a man who had committed a murder. When he arrived, he found that the offender had been so tightly trussed up with ropes for a number of days that one of the ropes had cut deeply into the man's arm. This had resulted in a septic accumulation. Charity prevailed over prudence, and Reggie took it upon himself to undo the bonds. The pus stored up in the abscess suddenly burst forth, splashed him, and passed on the infection. He was quickly a sick man himself, and was flown to hospital in Khartoum. For a time it looked as though the murderer was going to be responsible not merely for one death but for two.

He dismissed it all now as ancient history. The Isle of Wight, from which he had recently come on one of the small anachronistic paddle-boats that linked the island with Bournemouth and Swanage in summer, had been his father's choice for retirement, and Reggie had already benefited by a fortnight there. This was a good time of year for his leave. Swanage was at its best in early summer. Later, in August, the little town, highly popular as a family holiday-centre, always became over-crowded and it was our custom to let the bungalow and retreat to a remote district of Donegal in the west of Ireland. But in June and July Swanage was calculated to satisfy even the most critical.

I strove in vain to take Reggie on one or more of my many delightful morning rides. Of these I had a considerable repertoire. There was one which I took generally with younger children. We would go past the tennis courts and through the steep cutting on to the sea-front, a route never popular with the horses because, despite the raised level of the tarmac road, it took us immediately above the beach where the waves were quietly breaking. Our mounts seemed to feel themselves threatened. Tinker would fume and dance at every little wave which broke. Pop, the black pony, might go on strike and remain moodily motionless, until it was quite evident that we were not turning back to rejoin her. We would then ride past the Mowlem Institute, and through the town. This led to a great deal of dancing on the part of Tinker in the narrow street between the shops; but it was nice to be on a lively animal that showed off like a war-horse. Soon we were passing the Victoria Hotel with its fine late Georgian frontage and advancing towards the Grosvenor, a symbol of Edwardian security and comfort. Just beyond it, one looked down from the road leading out to Peveril Point to a quaint little two-storied house built in the garden of a larger red-brick domicile. In it lived an eccentric old gentleman who seemed to spend most of his time burning papers in the garden. When he vanished from the scene, the place was renovated and nearly doubled in size to be occupied by an invalid with a very pretty attendant. The invalid sat out in the garden, and the attendant, fortunately for me, often came out of the house. Perhaps she was not an attendant at all, but a hostess looking after a sick friend. But for a second or two, I used to share their lives as I rode by and was reassured to note that the invalid had a wicker armchair which was easy to move from one place to another. All this was set against a background of glittering, shimmering sea as one looked towards the distant chalky cliffs of the Isle of Wight, or at the green outline of Ballard Down across the blue, sunlit bay.

This ride was a mere trot through the town for beginners, followed perhaps by a canter up the green slope that mounted towards Durlston and that Mecca of day-tourists, the Swanage Globe. I would not have dreamt of taking Reggie on it. But there were other and more ambitious rides which he would have enjoyed and which would have kept us out for an hour-and-a-half or even two hours. There was the Dancing Ledge ride; out by Hirston, up past the quarries and along the Priest's Walk, its floor almost as stony as the gully of some stream, so that one guided one's mount up it as if in the Nevadas, sparing them as much stumbling and slipping as possible. Occasionally a shoe struck a spark out of a large rock embedded in the track. Presently we would reach a single lonely farm in a huge open field, and pass it. Not a habitation in sight now, not a sign of any other human being; a land of larks and perhaps a stray fox come to inhabit the cliffs. Even the horses seemed to share the excitement of this ride. The moment the last green stretch, known to us as the Race Track, was reached they would begin to fidget and snatch at the bit. The landscape seemed to produce some scenic fever in their blood as well as in ours. We, and they, were waiting for the moment when, having reached a low unmorticed wall, we would dismount and give their backs a rest. The ground sloped down from where we had halted to gaze out across half a mile of wild rough land, bramble clumps and coarse yellow grass, to where the edge of the low cliff began with the vast prospect of the English

Channel before it. With reins looped over our arms, we would stand silently behind the wall, breathing the freshness of the gorse-scented air and stare out to sea. As long as we did so, our mounts were content to wait. But the moment we passed the reins back over their heads, they were all impatience. They could hardly wait for us to get a foot into the stirrup, Lizzie, the ex-racehorse, backing and certain to be in a frenzy if kept another moment. I would be the last to swing myself into the saddle and back we would go, thundering up the rise, Tinker and his crony, the grey, Jimmy, threatening one another with bared teeth and capable even in their excitement of a playful kick if their riders allowed them to remain alongside for too long. It was their moment of elation as well as ours.

The Dancing Ledge ride was on the west side of the valley. But most of my best rides were to the east; on one or other of the two downs; or to Studland beach and along it almost as far as the ferry; or across the sandy, heather-covered moor to Agglestone Rock, using a tiny, narrow, very uneven foot-track — hardly that — on which the horses were liable to stumble. One of the nicest of all our routes was a great circular one, starting up Knitson Lane, crossing the road to descend on Rempstone Manor, and then circling its woods which harboured a small herd of deer. These were never seen by any of the children and only once by me, when I caught the flash of a doe's broad white stumpy tail flattened back against her fawn-coloured hindquarters as she galloped away between the trees. Beside a field-gate on the far side of the wood stood a great chestnut tree laden in autumn with eating chestnuts. Here the children would dismount, stuffing the pockets of their riding breeches or jodphurs with chestnuts. When these were full, they would force the chestnuts down into their woollen stockings so that their calves and shins bulged with strange eruptions as they rode home. Our return was across a corner of the moor and up a minute triangular green field where an old lady camped in summer, together with a Dalmatian dog, a tiny pony and a maid in trim cap and apron and blue linen dress. The maid, when she heard us coming, used to rush out from the tent and hold the pony by the picket rope as we rode by. Although the tranquil pony never showed the smallest sign of excitement, this precaution was always taken.

These and other rides of an equally delightful nature awaited

Reggie's pleasure. But he refused them all saying that he had no suitable clothes and disliked riding in flannel slacks. In a last effort to break his resistance I formed a plan to produce my pupil as an incentive.

"You can take the ride instead of me, Reggie. I will give you only experienced riders, and you can borrow my riding-breeches if you can get into them. Try them on while I'm up at the school at breakfast."

Anne had been given a course of six rides as a birthday present by a god-mother or by some relative. I said nothing to her of my plan, but at breakfast I told her to come down to the bungalow ahead of the others when I would explain to her what was happening.

"Yes, you may ride Tinker. But bring him down before you saddle up. I want to make sure that his rubbed shoulder is all right."

I saw her through the window of the end room of our bungalow as she rode up. My elaborate scheme had come to nothing for our guest had silently refused all my blandishments to take charge of the ride. As I walked towards the door I chose, without thinking about it, the largest strawberry from a bowl on the small table under the window. I went down the cement path, past the fruit net to where Anne was seated bare-back on Tinker outside the little green wicket-gate. Concealing behind my back what I had brought, I said to her,

"Shut your eyes and open your mouth and see what luck will bring you."

I had not used the phrase since childhood but it came to hand now as obediently as a peregrine to the wrist of a falconer. She looked amused but did as directed. I laid a hand on Tinker's neck, and, reaching up, pressed the crimson fruit against her lips.

"You mustn't thank me!"

To play out my subterfuge I gave the horse's shoulder a short examination, and then told her to ride back to the farm and saddle up. The whole episode occupied a minute of time or less. But that moment when I held the strawberry by its green stalk up to her lips which she accepted with closed eyes remains vividly fixed in my mind, as vividly fixed as Rousseau's memory of climbing a cherry tree and throwing down bunches of cherries into the laps of his two companions waiting below.

My plot had failed over the ride, and was nearly to fail in another endeavour to give entertainment to our guest by getting him to accompany us to the half-term dance. By now he had been with us several days. He already knew a number of our colleagues from previous visits. He attended the Sunday concert and remained to supper; and he came to the school play, where a brilliantly clever fourteen-year-old boy whose mother was French played Argan in *Le Malade Imaginaire*, giving us a perfect stage representation of a valetudinarian, with all the invalid's nervous irritability, his querulousness, his moments of fussy and angry self-assertion followed by sudden and self-pitying collapse, his impotent attempts to lean his stick against the arm of his chair, his impatience over trifles, the martyred expression on his face as the pillows were being arranged behind his head, the sniffings and snuffings and sudden violent spasms of nose-blowing, as though he had a grudge against his own handkerchief, the amazing deliberation with which he placed himself in or removed himself from his chair, the first hesitating steps, leaning heavily upon the handle of his stick, and the shuffling progress as he began to move about the room – all these were enacted realistically and without ever descending to the burlesque.

Anne's father and mother were at the play and were amongst the parents to whom I introduced our guest. Reggie, as I have said, was not unsociable. His manners were friendly and natural, but there was a fundamental degree of reserve which was probably self-chosen. He hated being run after, though most women who met him found it hard not to fall a little in love with him. It was a waste of time on their part. All they would get was the unfailing courtesy of a well-mannered undergraduate. He had the slight detachment of someone who has spent too much of his time in distant places with only natives to speak to. I was seeing as much as I could of him in the intervals of my various classes and assignments. He was free to come up to the school whenever he felt like it. His reluctance to attend the dance was overcome by our insistence that it would be regarded as an act of deliberate incivility to the Old Lady.

"It will be unkind to the children too, not to come. They love a few strange faces. There will be quite a lot of parents at the dance and a number of them are from overseas. You will have plenty to talk about."

I have told you how much I enjoyed the school dances, even
those at the end of term; but the mid-term dance had no cares
preceding it except for those occupied with the school play. It was
a delightful social occasion.

I preceded my wife and Reggie up to the school for supper.
When I got there, the Old Lady was not yet in her place at the
head of the table. She appeared shortly. The success of Molière's
play had pleased her for she had been Jo's right-hand in its
production. Reggie and my wife arrived as supper ended. They
had supped at the bungalow. We had brought our horse to the
water but it looked as though he would refuse to drink. He had
from the first announced that there was no question of his dancing.

"I am the man with two left feet. And, in any case, I have only
these walking shoes. . . ."

It seemed best to maintain a pretence of accepting his ruling,
though when the evening had warmed up, I introduced him to a
fifteen-year-old red-head, the best dancer in the room, who
would have been able to steer a rhinoceros through the intricacies
of the waltz on a first meeting. He came through the ordeal
successfully and was then made briefly to partner the little fairy-
like Helen Tasker, who had been left deserted.

"Now you must dance with Anne."

It was a polka of all things. But they survived it and, looking
across the room when it ended, I saw them talking together side
by side. She was viewing him with some degree of admiration,
which was only to be expected. What was truly miraculous was
that when the music struck up once more, they danced the next
dance together. This concluded Reggie's dancing for the
evening. I experienced a mixture of amusement and gratification
at having achieved as much as I had. My feelings were those of a
ringmaster who has successfully put a particularly difficult tiger
through a hoop. They had danced together twice. It gave me
genuine pleasure that he should be struck by her uniqueness. I
wanted him to like her. He seemed a most suitable object for her
affection. If, in his impregnable stronghold, my brother-in-law
was in some degree susceptible to her charm – and the very word
seems in itself to do her immediate injustice – was it any wonder
that some female members of the staff saw her as *une fille fatale*?

The dance ended as always with Sir Roger de Coverly. When its rather lengthy and repetitive manoeuvres were concluded, hands were joined, a large circle formed, and Auld Lang Syne was sung. But before that a rather curious incident took place. When I danced with Anne I learnt from her that this would be her last school dance. She was leaving early, a few days before the end of term. She had to go home for some reason or other. And suddenly, and absurdly, I felt a sense of strong personal grievance. Pupils should not leave before the end of term to suit their own convenience. They should not be allowed to cut any of the social functions which help to keep a school community together.

I felt this, even though at the same time I had become a match-maker. You have seen a child pressing the last slice on the plate upon a visitor. With one part of their being, they quite genuinely want them to take it. I was like that. Here were two people whom I liked. It was fitting they should like each other. The friendship might easily develop. Reggie's leave would last into August, and he would be with his father at Bonchurch when we visited the latter briefly before going to Donegal. Bonchurch was only a few miles from Niton, and it had been with entirely innocent good-will and on the impulse of the moment that I had said to Anne towards the close of the evening,

"Good news for you, Anne! The handsome Reggie will still be in the Isle of Wight when you go there in August."

Miss Whitworth was standing nearby and she could hear what I said. So could my wife, who murmured to me when Anne had gone,

"I could never tease anyone like that. And in front of Miss Whit too!"

"Tease her? But I like Anne! I'm one of her admirers myself."

"I know that. That's just what I mean."

But what did she mean? To this day, I do not know. That cryptic utterance continues to baffle me. Nothing easier than to ask; but I never did, probably because I did not want an explanation. It was not because of our agreed reticence, already mentioned, in such matters. It was, I believe, the remote possibility – so remote that it would have been like a drowning man clutching a straw, that she might reply,

"Anne is fond of you. And it is therefore not fair to tease her about someone else in a spirit which seems to imply that it does not matter a hang to you who else is or is not a recipient of her approval."

Anne's mother, who was at the dance, invited us to bring Reggie over to tea next day when the school started its half-term week-end of freedom. Her husband taught at Bryanston, and, during the term, they lived in a pleasant secluded house in the woods near Blandford, a few miles from the school. Their other home was at Niton in the Isle of Wight near Freshwater, and it was amusing to discover later that Reggie, whose parents also lived in the island, and Anne's father were not, as they imagined, meeting for the first time. Their paths had crossed once before when Reggie, on leave at the time, had gone over to Freshwater to purchase a yacht which Anne's father had for sale.

At three o'clock, we set off for Blandford in the car, looking forward to the drive quite as much as to the picnic tea which was to follow. Asked which of the many buildings seen in the course of my nomadic life stands out most clearly in memory, I believe I would name not the Parthenon; not St. Peter's; not the Wurzburg Residence or Bruhl in all their disciplined baroque assurance without, and all their fantastic imaginative wealth within; but I would choose Corfe Castle, that broken ruin with its two sharply-silhouetted, shattered fragments of unequal height on their green cone in the narrow gap between the broken lengths of chalky down. The destroyed castle, and I suspect it is equally true of the Parthenon, has gained from its overthrow. Now it dominates the landscape for miles round in a unique way. It is like a concentrate of history tied up into a single phrase. As well as Corfe, our drive that day gave us the long stretch of moor to Wareham, followed by the even wilder-looking moorland extending to Bere Regis, all of it country immortalised by Hardy. But I can do without Hardy. I don't need his Wessex. I prefer my own more recent Dorset in which I spent twelve such happy years.

Anne had explained to us how to find their home hidden in the depths of a copse and completely isolated, even though only a mile or two out of Blandford town. The whole occasion is slightly blurred in my memory. I know that we praised their little wood while secretly preferring our own open meadows, gorse, and stubble fields; and that we helped to carry out tea to rugs spread in the spangled shade of a group of birch trees. I know too that the afternoon did not seem to have advanced to any extent my activities in the role of match-maker. It was Anne's mother, the poet of the family, who, when an opportunity occurred, launched forth to my wife in a rhapsody on the subject of her brother's good-looks, to which she seemed to have fallen a complete victim.

Anne herself was in one of her misanthropic moods. She was silent for most of the time and seemed to be avoiding us all, Reggie included. It was her younger sister who took us to show us the beauties of the wood. I know that I draw extremely superficial inferences from the behaviour of other people, while subjecting my own to the most searching analysis. I interpreted her aloofness now, not to indifference, but quite possibly to youthful dread of admitting even to herself that our Adonis was making any impression on her. In all likelihood, she recovered her poise, and some of her sardonic spirit, once back amongst her school-fellows, and made a jest of the whole business. At school-tea, a few days later, I learned from Joan Wilson that they had all been ragging her unmercifully, searching for possible rhymes to "Reggie" in case she should feel inclined to celebrate him metri-cally, and pointing out that there was a distinct paucity of suitable words and that she should be duly grateful for their efforts to find some for her. All of which, according to Joan, she took in good part.

The picnic had achieved nothing. The calm of the impervious Reggie had in no way been disturbed. Nor had Anne shown any signs of maidenly distress. But how wrong one can be in such assessments. One at least of the two had not remained entirely unaffected. And it was the one whom I would have least suspec-ted.

I thought my brother-in-law impervious. But I was wrong. In my father's study when I was a child was a barometer which wrote with a pen upon an unwinding scroll of squared paper the sudden peaks and the equally sudden descents in climatic variations which took place over the weeks. There are one or two charts of my own emotional life where the pen has had to mount to sudden heights. But in Reggie's case, I would have said that the line never varied in any great degree from the horizontal "Set Fair". And it surprised me to learn, as I presently did, that in actual fact the chart showed his emotions behaving in an unaccustomed fashion.

It was from my wife I learned this, and only some months later. She told me that Reggie was attracted to Anne. He wanted to know was he too old for her? Or, rather, would he be too old by the time she had grown up and he was free to marry? Actually the period of waiting was about the same; that is to say, it entailed not more than three years in either case. There are numerous individuals who have been kept waiting a great deal longer than that for married happiness. My wife pointed out that in her opinion time was less important than the differences in their respective tastes, and in the conditions of life which would await Anne if she went out to the Sudan. She would have to give up all her ambitions in music. Even if promotion were to take him to Khartoum, she would be buried away from nearly everything which she valued most in life. Her career would be finished before it ever began; and it was doubtful that his career would be of sufficient interest to her to compensate for the loss of her own.

Reggie agreed. He confided that he felt a ten-years' difference in age was a lot. Add to that the other consideration, which have been mentioned, and the whole idea quickly began to appear silly and selfish.

In many ways I am glad that I was not aware of this discussion. Had I been consulted I believe the romantic in me would have prevailed and I would have encouraged the friendship. To do so would probably have been wrong. Reggie was already wedded to a stern partner – duty. And when he did marry – incidentally to someone even younger than Anne – it needed much courage and understanding on both sides to make the marriage a happy one.

Now that I think about it, I realise my wife's advice was sound. Everything she said was true. She loved her brother and she had nothing but good-will for Anne. She wished them both well. I am pretty certain her assessment was astute and correct.

Reggie remained a day or two more with us and then returned to his widowed father in the Isle of Wight. We parted with the reassuring thought that we would meet again before long. The summer term resumed its hectic course. There was tennis, the annual verse-speaking examination of the Poetry Society, the Royal Drawing Society competition, week-end camps for the Girl Guides, the Scouts, and even the Cubs, and of course the daily sea-bathe, from the two outsize, linked bathing huts raised on stilts on the narrow strip of beach immediately below the promenade. A school raft lay anchored about seventy yards out from the shore and a tiny, flat-bottomed dinghy, manned by a member of the staff or by a senior boy, was paddled around the raft in case any swimmer got into difficulties. This dinghy, which would have turned turtle had anyone laid so much as a finger on its gunwale, had to be carried up at the end of the bathe. It resided then for another twenty-three hours on two stout wooden bars pushed into slots underneath the two, huge, adjoining bathing huts. The senior boys had to carry it up from the wave's edge and lift it into position. This brings to mind one of the very few occasions on which I resorted to personal violence. One day, when it was my function to supervise them, I lost my temper utterly when repeated calls had failed to collect a quota from the various individuals dawdling on the sands or kicking a beach-ball about. I called up all the designated boat-handlers and ordered them to await me up at the school before lunch. There I gave them each two with a gym-shoe. Better this than an endless sequence of further expostulations. It never happened again. They came when called and I was saved all further frustration.

Though the days were packed with a succession of activities, which was what the Old Lady and Arthur wanted, I never felt harassed beyond endurance. I lived in an atmosphere of culture, with interesting friends outside the school and agreeable colleagues inside it. Quite apart from our bungalow, I enjoyed reasonable privacy of mind at the school; not perhaps during the rest period when I was kept busy winding the handle of the E.M.G. to furnish agreeable sounds through its huge papiermâché horn, but certainly on my rides with the children when I had a feeling of owning the earth, or at least as much of it as any reasonable individual had a right to demand.

Anne was drawing near the close of her six riding lessons. She had been given good value for her money. But in this she was very far from being an exception. Arthur knew perfectly well that I was as generous with his horseflesh as with my own time. He himself, when he took a lesson, frequently did the same. I have seen him return from a morning ride almost as late for his class as I so frequently did.

Anne had had the best of the Knitson rides, of Studland beach, of the downs, and of the wooded environs of Rempstone Manor. On her last ride but one, we made a new discovery. I was under the impression that I knew every track, every bridle-path, every ride within a distance of five miles. But in this I was wrong. The Spencer-Watsons were giving another mime-show in two days' time. I wanted to tell them that there was no chance of my coming to the evening performance. It was on Wednesday when I would be on duty in the evening. There was just a chance I might be able to get to the afternoon matinée. I collected the two students who were due for their lesson, and we rode out along the valley road towards Harmon's Cross. I was always loth to trot on a tarmac surface, having learnt in the army how fatal French cobbles could be to a horse's legs. Tinker's had been damaged by his previous owner's carelessness, and we had to be careful to prevent "splints" from developing. I decided to try and find another route. We turned down a farm lane after the Langton Matravers juncture and soon the ground fell away in front of us as we descended into one of those bowls to be found on the far side of the valley road. Presently we came to a dour grey little farmhouse and rode stealthily past, thanking our good luck that there were no barking dogs to bring out the farmer in protest against our trespass on his land. After that fortune favoured us. Steering mainly by guess-work, we found a track through fields and along hedges until we plunged at last into a large copse where, with the track shielded from the sun by numerous silver-stemmed young birches, a few very late bluebells still lingered. A green woodpecker flitted in a series of uneven rises and falls between the trees. We caught a glimpse of its bright red crest and heard its protesting voice. We smelt garlic and, presently, bracken, and then a sudden over-whelming scent of elder flower. The turf under our horses' feet was soft and spongy, not with the rain of winter but with the dry mosses and crumbled humus of mid-summer. At last we emerged from the copse and found ourselves at the back of the two labourers' cottages opposite the brief stretch of private road down to Dunshay.

It was half-past nine and Hilda and Mary were enjoying a late breakfast under a walnut tree on the lawn. They had been up at seven, but there had been goats and cows and the young Jersey bull, and the grey mules, and the horses, and the dogs all to be thought of before themselves. As soon as breakfast was over, rehearsing would begin and would go on till lunch time. A spot-ted Dalmatian lay on the lawn beside them. It got up when it saw us and trotted to meet us, far too intelligent and courteous to bark at any one who had the good sense and taste to arrive on horse-back.

"Hullo! Early morning visit from our poet! And you've brought Anne with you!"

"Yes. I've brought Anne and Rosaleen. But we'll have to be quick. I've a class at half-past ten."

We were talking over the top of the low garden-wall, which separated the lawn from the avenue and the great, circular pond, skirted by a parapet except for one sloping ingress, the pond into which Hilda and Mary rode the horses and mules bareback when they watered them.

"Hold Lizzie for me, will you, Rosaleen?"

I slipped off her back. At one side of this second entrance gate were two stone steps and a mounting block which was probably there when the Spanish Armada set sail for England.

"Won't you have breakfast with us?"

"I've had it already."

"A cup of coffee then?"

"That would be lovely, if you don't think it will make my escort too jealous."

Mary went to the house and returned with a huge cup and saucer brought back from the south of France. On the side of the cup were emblazoned the words, "*En amour les apprentices en savent autant que les maîtres.*" This profoundly psychological dictum was a reminder that peasant sagacity can put the intellectual in his place when it comes to the basic emotions. As I drank my coffee I thought, "I don't want my apprenticeship ever to end; but I suppose it must someday."

"I can't come on Wednesday night. I'm on duty. But I'm going to try and wangle Wednesday afternoon. It's a half-holiday and there are two matches being played, so I don't think I'll be needed for a junior game."

"You must come. We particularly want you. Shall we tell him the secret, Mary?"

Mary nodded.

"We're doing a poem of yours."

"What poem?"

"We won't tell you. You must come and find out for yourself."

This was distinctly tantalising. I drank the huge cup of creamy coffee. Then Mary was sent on another message, to fetch a box of chocolates from the house and to offer them to my companions.

"Bad horsemanship to let them graze with their bits in, but I don't want any delay."

"Why don't you bring Anne with you on Wednesday? And this

young woman," turning to Rosaleen.

It was amusing to see how the two faces lit up for an instant at the suggestion.

"It's an idea. But I don't think it's possible."

"Oh, we could, sir. I'm sure we could."

"But haven't you a tennis match?"

"Blow! I'd forgotten," exclaimed Rosaleen.

"Dosie has, but I haven't. It's the second six who are playing."

Dosie was the unflattering name by which Rosaleen, well-beloved by everybody in the school, was known to her best friends.

"I don't think there's much chance. But I'll think it over. I know you'd love the show, Anne. If I think there's any hope, I will make the suggestion."

Mary joined us at the gate in her huge, multi-coloured, coarsely-plaited straw hat, and the chocolates were passed round. We rode back quickly, winding our way through the copse, cantering wherever there was an opportunity, and reaching the school just in time to take the horses down to the New Land, unsaddle them, and leave the saddles to dry along the top of the wooden gate before dashing into class. Later in the day I spoke to the Old Lady about the Wednesday proposal.

"You say that Mrs. Spencer-Watson specially asked her?"

"Yes. You see she knows Anne already. She and her mother have been over there with us for a poetry reading."

"Isn't she in any of the matches?"

"No, the first six aren't playing tomorrow. I tell you what I can do. We can combine business with pleasure. I'm behindhand with my riding lessons. There are so many taking them this term. I can make it a riding lesson for Anne at the same time. If we start early we can go over the down and by Harmon's Cross. Altogether she'll get at least an hour's riding."

"I suppose it's all right. We seem to be always making concessions to that young lady. Sometimes it's her parents. Sometimes it's you."

"I think it will mean a lot to her."

"I'm sure it will. I wanted very much to go myself, but Jo and I have a meeting of the Guide Commissioners at Wimbourne."

"I'll say nothing to Anne yet. I've told her I'll let her know when Wednesday morning comes."

"Yes, perhaps that's wisest."

Wednesday came, and when I went up to breakfast Anne was still lingering at the table.

"Any luck, sir?"

"What right have you to expect luck?"

She smiled. I had said enough to arouse hope.

I left her in a state of anxiety for a moment and then admitted,

"Yes, every luck. At two o'clock this afternoon you are having a riding lesson. You are still due one more of your half-dozen, and it is becoming quite a problem how to fit it in. This afternoon, we go out by Knitson, up onto the down and as far along Nine Barrow Down as our wisdom sees fit to take us. Then we turn down towards Harmon's Cross and by a curious coincidence we find ourselves at the gate of Dunshay just ten minutes before a mime show, of which you may have heard rumours, is due to begin. Our horses are sweating. They are obviously tired by their gallop over the downs, and we shall have to decide what action is best to take in the circumstances. Don't grin. Perhaps I shall decide to walk them home. Thank your headmistress and tell your nearest and dearest friends, if you like, but don't bleat about it all over the school: there are other people interested in miming as well as you, who don't ride, and who haven't the luck of knowing Mrs. Spencer-Watson. There is no point in making them envious."

A smile of delight spread across her face and she went off to tell Joan. I was just rising from the table when she returned.

"Won't I look rather odd in riding breeches this afternoon? Joan says she's always heard their shows are so fashionable."

"If you will look odd in riding breeches, I will look just as odd, and perhaps even odder. Two oddities are preferable to one; they will keep each other in countenance."

"I suppose it would be quite absurd to bring a dress and change?"

"Yes, absolutely absurd and besides it would give a lot of trouble. May I remind you that, on this occasion, you are going to look at rather than be looked at."

"Why are you so horrid always?"

"Because it is deeply engrained in my nature. I am cruel, malicious, vindictive, spiteful, arrogant, of great cunning, easily moved to vengeance, and diabolically clever in thinking out new ways of injuring those whom I pretend to serve. I have been known to hit a pupil on the head with the Encyclopaedia Britannica so that they passed into an immediate coma out of which they did not come for six weeks."

I said this. But what I really wanted to say was, "Bring a dress, by all means; bring that silk, flower-patterned dress which you wore when I was "taking tea" up at the school last week, and which suits your brown hair, and the flat metal band you wear across it. Put the dress, a comb, and the metal hair band in a paper bag and I will carry it for you. They weigh nothing. Then if I grow tired looking at the mimes, I can always look at you."

I could not imagine myself making such a speech in a thousand years. My lips were incapable of it. And yet my mind made it. My mind makes it even now. This is what our emotions do to us. They make madmen of us. To carry any other pupil's dress would have been merely a damned nuisance, especially on that rocking ship-of-the-desert, Lizzie. But to carry the dress that she was to wear later in the afternoon would have been a wonderful privilege. The magic that surrounds someone's *persona* can impart itself to everything that touches them, or that they may touch. Personality is holy. All life is holy as far as that goes. But we forget it, or only remember it when we fall in love. Then, by some strange aberration, we extend our reverence to everything connected with the loved one.

Immediately after lunch I slipped away, cutting out coffee and making my way down to the dark stable at the farm. The saddles were on their racks at the back of the stalls. Each of our mounts had a different response to girthing. Wendy would put back her ears and snap. Cobweb would stagger sideways as though she were about to collapse. Pop's multi-coloured girth could hardly be made to meet round her fat tummy. And Lizzie, versed in a well-known device, would blow out her belly so that I generally had to return to her a second time and, catching her unaware, pull up the strap another three or four holes.

"Get up, Liz. Get over, girl."

I pushed her forcibly to one side of the narrow stall to allow me to get past with the saddle. I had almost finished saddling, and was just tightening up the girths on Tinker, when Anne appeared in the brilliant sunlight of the doorway, barely able to see me in the darkness, but sun-gilded and sun-aureoled herself.

"Sorry. You've been doing all the work."

"That's all right."

She was wearing a white open-necked blouse, and beltless, well-cut jodpurs. Even in this uninspiring garb, she was different from anyone else; not necessarily prettier, but, for some reason, infinitely more significant; not more energetic, but ever so much more alive. She had only to speak for you to feel that life in her welled up from some deeper source. Her voice cut through the drowsy July air with an agreeable incision of its own, a voice wedded from childhood to a note of slight disdain, as though she felt obliged to give the lie in some way to the gentleness with which her animated grey eyes looked out on the world. It would have been pleasant to be going this afternoon to Dunshay with any of my pupils; it was a hundred-fold more pleasant to be going with her.

"You may ride Tinker."

"Oh, you are good."

"I will bucket along behind you on the well-meaning Liz. Cantering is her very worst pace. She throws you up in the saddle and forward, as though you were a sack of meal."

"Stop! You make me feel I'm being accompanied by a martyr."

"I am a martyr. But martyrdom has its own warm glow of satisfaction. Anne, we have exactly forty-five minutes to get to Dunshay and to slip into our seats before the performance begins."

I had changed my plans. We would come home by the downs and go the way I had discovered the other morning. Getting onto the down and off again would take too much time. Even if we went all out along the top, the preliminaries would neutralise any gain. We slipped out by Godlinstone, crossed the valley road, and walked the horses rather quietly past the uncurtained windows of the melancholy little farm, lest the owner or his wife should come out and tell us that we were unwelcome.

"Rein that impatient little devil Tinker in a bit, and listen to me. This is the first Spencer-Watson show you have seen. The Philistines find it hard to stifle their laughter on these occasions. All they can see is Hilda striding about barefooted on a concrete floor, striking a lot of strange attitudes, and Mary, in equally funny clothes, doing her best to keep up with her."

"Why do you tell me all this? I am not a Philistine."

"No, you're not a Philistine, and I don't expect your reactions to be those of Philistia. But you need to be prepared. You're going to hear poetry rendered visible as well as audible. If they dance 'The Waves', you will see two figures moving rhythmically to and fro across the back of the stage with an occasional dipping movement; figures against a Botticelli background with a touch of dark-crimsoned Medici splendour added by their costumes. Their tilted heads, their curved arms, their undulating sequences of movements repeated again and again, will, to the Philistines, seem quite incomprehensible and even a little absurd. But to the rest of us, they will reveal exactly what Mozart meant his music to convey, even though he may not have been thinking about waves at all."

The avenue gate of Dunshay, in deep shade at the bottom of a short, steep pitch of hill, stood widely open. The notice "Please telephone before you come," had been removed.

Near the house the farmhand was getting cars to turn around the pond, deposit their passengers in front of the theatre just above, and then withdraw to a paddock amongst trees on the far side of the avenue.

"We're all right, Anne. We're to leave Tinker and Liz in the stable. Their horses will be out."

It was pleasant to come in out of the blinding sunlight into the cool of the cobbled stable, to unsaddle the horses and leave them attached to the heavy iron manger by a neckstrap, and then to slip quickly across the garden and up past the pond to the door of the barn where one of Hilda's many faithful adherents was checking tickets and distributing the long narrow printed cards which bore the programme.

Most of the faithful were already gathered, the women garbed in their gayest summer attire and fanning themselves with their cards, the men with a resolute expression which seemed to say, "This is culture and we have got to go through with it, but how wonderful if will be when we get outside once more and can light a cigarette." Two of the English Singers, Norman Notley and David Bryndley, were chatting happily with Archie Russell, connoisseur and expert on Blake. An arty-crafty young woman with a pleasant smile helped us to find places.

"There's a seat on the bench in front at the far end of the row, and" – turning to Anne – "perhaps you could manage with a cushion?"

"You take the seat, Anne. I'll sit on the floor."

"No please. I like the floor. Honestly!"

So for the next hour-and-a-half, I sat with my head tilted against the whitewashed further wall of the theatre, with Anne at my feet, curled up on an immense, spread-eagled cushion. She leaned back against the bench, her shoulder just touching my knee. I had the double pleasure of watching what was happening on the stage and at the same time getting an occasional glimpse of the effect it was having from the face of my companion. She was the last link in that long line of subtle communication which extends from the creative mind through the interpretative artist to the receiving subject. Her lips were slightly parted, her face wore that expression which I knew so well, that air of impassioned reproach to life for being at once so beautiful and so anguished.

The programme was as good as any that I had seen in the thatched theatre. A sequence to music by Mussorgsky depicted the alternations of violence and peace in men's lives. A group of Elizabethan lyrics were exquisitely sung from behind a side curtain by the invisible Rose Morse. Then followed the group of three poems in which I had been told I would find a personal interest. Hilda appeared, tall, and gaunt, and wearing what was really more like a dunce's cap than anything else. She and Mary both wore male costumes of a freakish anonymity. In a clear voice Rose Morse recited the poems from behind a screen. Her invisibility gave full force to the words, yet allowed attention to concentrate on the mime. We heard Blake's reflections on "This life's five windows of the soul", and AE's upon the vestures of that soul.

> I pitied one whose tattered dress
> Was patched, and stained with dust and rain;
> He smiled on me; I could not guess
> The viewless spirit's wide domain.

> He said, "The royal robe I wear
> Trails all along the fields of light:
> Its silent blue and silver bear
> For gems the starry dust of night. . . ."

Finally came my own little poem, "Gods".

> The gods are dead they tell us now,
> None walk the earth as they once did.

Yet each may be a god who wills,
And none prevent him, none forbid.

A penny given to a child
Can turn a sky of grey to gold;
Two pennies given make his heart
Leap with the joy of wealth untold.

Now am I Mercury, if I wish.
Now am I Zeus, if I so choose.
Now can I bring Olympus down
To this next mortal lacking shoes.

He passes me, the chance is gone,
The god's wing'd feet o'er-look his need;
Olympus clouds again with mist:
What men proclaim is true indeed.

The two dancers with their cone-shaped headgear had become
Olympians walking this earth with heavenly confidence, now with
long strides and now with mincing paces. The tall Hilda was
presumably Zeus and Mary his companion Mercury. They distributed largesse to certain invisible and needy mortals. It was all
very strange, and curiously effective. But Hilda, as I learnt later
when talking to her on the lawn, had worked on an entirely
esoteric interpretation of her own. My lines seemed crystal clear
to me: but she had found something else in them; it was not very
easy to say exactly what. It did not matter. The poem was beauti-
fully recited and the audience seemed pleased. I was willing to
bow before the superiority of her intuition and to believe that
perhaps my poem should really have meant what she in her
sagacity had decided it ought to mean!

Finally, we had what I loved so well and what, for Anne's sake, I
had been praying we might have: "Walk, Shepherdess, Walk." A
hidden voice translated us for a few brief instants to the border-
land of the Golden Age, where all living creatures are happy, and
where there is nothing to temper the zest with which a human
being responds to living. Equipped with crooks, wearing little
straw hats with curved brims, and garbed in elaborate, much-be-
ribboned, lovely and yet almost absurd Arcadian costumes, with
the flounce of the shepherdess's short skirt looped back to reveal
the petticoat, they danced to Eleanor Farjeon's thrice-repeated
quatrain:-

Walk, shepherdess, walk, and I'll walk too,
To find the ram with the ebony horn and the gold-footed ewe.
The lamb with the fleece of silver like summer sea's foam,
The wether with the crystal bell that leads them all home.

Eleanor Farjeon, the writer of the lines, had composed the music too. Words and tune were perfectly wedded. One felt that Mary, instead of those crossed arms, should really be carrying a kid from one of the white goats outside. Everything they did was a blend of rural simplicity and mannered artifice. Rose Morse's lovely voice rang clearly through the little theatre with a lilt that was visually embodied in the succession of quick, gliding, formally-patterned movements of the two dancers to and fro across the stage, a lean, Lovat Fraser shepherd and a shepherdess, flushed with all the joy of spring.

The applause died away. Several stiff and slightly-relieved individuals rose from their seats and felt hopefully for their cigarette cases. The audience of about forty poured out, into the strong sunlight outside. Mary, still in her shepherdess costume, opened the stage-door of the barn and called to us that we were to make our way to the lawn where we would find tea waiting for us.

"Strawberries and cream, Anne. A pity you don't like them!"

She was too old to be teased in this fashion. She looked at me in pitying scorn as if to say, "Please don't be so infantile." As we made our way on to the manor lawn, a facetious acquaintance, noticing our riding breeches, said to me,

"What! Are we to have a rodeo to follow?!"

Gravitating towards a figure familiar to us both, we found May Gilbert, a former member of staff of the school, seated beneath a quince tree which offered precious little shade but great promise of future fruit.

When she realised that Anne was from the school, she demanded, "Why is this young woman so singularly favoured?"

"Firstly, because she is a riding pupil owed several lessons, and the term is getting short. Secondly, because she happened to be with me when we rode over here the other morning and Mrs. Spencer-Watson invited her. Thirdly, because she's a young person of sense and good feeling and as likely to enjoy it as anyone I know. Are you satisfied?"

She professed herself satisfied, but Anne protested against my choice of words.

"I don't like being 'a young person'. You sound like a policeman giving evidence in court."

"So I am. The young person, if you want to know, Miss Gilbert, is idle, scatter-brained, unable to concentrate, and generally suspicious of anything in the nature of hard work. She is extremely unpopular with her companions about whom she tells tales which are generally quite without foundation. Her spelling is execrable and her riding is even worse. She has been warned repeatedly that if –"

". . . she is teased any more she will burst into loud, hysterical sobs."

"Don't, I implore you, Anne. Have some strawberries and cream instead."

It was half-past five when we left. Slipping away to the stable, we saddled the horses and received an acclamation from the rest of the guests when we re-appeared riding them. Both our mounts rose to the occasion; Tinker, reined in by his competent rider, pranced along with impatient little steps and presently broke into a miniature canter. And Lizzie pricked her ears, threw up her head and behaved exactly as though I was taking her out of the paddock down to the starting point at Epsom.

It was an appropriate ending to a perfect afternoon. We rode out on the grass margin towards the avenue gate, saluted by the farm labourer, who was about to close it before turning the cows out after milking. The narrow road leading back to Harmon's Cross breathed honeysuckle; a great, bristling, reddish boar rose in his heavily-strawed pen at the farm in the lane beyond, placed his two front trotters on the wall of the sty and inspected us as we came through the yard. Under the elms ahead a group of cows had taken refuge from the flies; a late cuckoo called from the copse a little further on; the sharp yap of a young dog greeted us at the end of the lane; and presently we were leaning forward in the saddle, with reins loose and patting the damp sweaty necks of our mounts as they scrambled up the narrow chalky track on to the down. There the air was fresher; a breeze coming from the north brought – or seemed to bring with the imaginative aid of the vast panorama spreading towards the ferry road – a breath of salty sea air which lingered in the nostrils until extinguished by the smell of great clumps of gorse. We gathered up our reins as we felt the tightening of muscle and the quickening of excitement in the living creatures beneath us, proof that they too welcomed the prospect of the long, flat stretch of down ahead.

I have few recollections of the remaining half of that term. I know that it was one of the finest summers that we had experienced for years. An urgent invitation from great friends in Donegal took my wife and our young children off to Ireland at the beginning of July. I would join them there later after first paying a visit to my father-in-law at his Bonchurch home, "Sunnybrae", on the island. I was alone at the bungalow, though in weather as idyllic as we were having it was difficult to feel deserted. I would come out in the morning shortly before eight o' clock, on my way to breakfast at the school, smell the gorse and see the green outline of Ballard Down thrown into relief against a sky which had ceased to be milky and in an hour or so would have become deepest blue. The two farm horses, Sally, a magnificent strawberry roan, half-a-ton or more of well-bred Clydesdale, and her recently arrived partner Betty, almost as huge and quite as impressive, had not yet been summoned to work, and were still grazing in their field to the left of the lane which led towards the farm and then on up to the school. They were giants both of them. Their great hairy fetlocks used to ring out on the cobbles near the stable like successive blows of a sledge-hammer. Nevertheless, I have seen Betty clear in one flying bound the metal water-trough on its wooden stand, which formed a substitute for the fencing in the lane corner of their enclosure. It was a jump of at least three-and-a-half feet by this cantering mastodon, who had got into a flurry because she had been left out alone.

The fifth form were occupied with their certificate examination. That may be why I have practically no memories of Anne in those closing weeks. I was busy. She was busy. In less than no time – an absurd phrase, almost equal in its deliberate absurdity to that of my nurse when she ordered us as children to do something "immediately, if not sooner" – she would have passed out of the picture. As each generation of pupils in the school moved on, one had the feeling that a particular phase of one's own life had also ended. One must just begin rebuilding all over again in mid-September. When that brilliant sixth form left, it was as though a whole constellation had disappeared from the sky. Anne's departure, if one wished to be rhetorical, was more like the effacement of a single star. I thought of Browning's little poem, "My Star."

All that I know
  Of a certain star
Is, it can throw
  (Like an angled spar)
Now a dart of red,
  Now a dart of blue;
Till my friends have said
  They would fain see, too,
My star that dartles the red and blue!
Then it stops like a bird; like a flower hangs furled:
They must solace themselves with the Saturn above it.
What matter to me if their star is a world?
Mine has opened its soul for me; therefore I love it.

Anne, on the contrary, never opened her soul to me. Once, that day at the end of tea, she seemed on the verge of doing so, and I gave her what help I could. But it was nothing. Like the angled spar, something in her gave forth varied colours and we were dazzled by them. I look now at her exercise book and there is nothing really very special, even in her paraphrase of Shelley's poem. In it she betrays essentially her depth of feeling, that depth against which irony was her only defence. Least of all my pupils could I flatter myself that I had armed her against life. All I did was to applaud a sensibility which might make her desperately unhappy in the end. And yet I felt it would have been an even greater crime against emergent personality to have discouraged it.

If someone had asked me at any time during those years, "What do you want for her?", I could truthfully have replied, "I want her to be happy." "Nothing else?" "Well, I would like to be the occasional witness of her happiness." I never asked for – or even, I believe, desired to any real extent – her affection. Apart from everything else, that would have been the direct road to unhappiness, as far as she was concerned. Nevertheless, a part of me, although it did not actually hunger for it, would have been reassured to know that some shadow of such a feeling existed. If Charlotte Brontë could fall passionately in love with her bearded professor in Brussels, it was not beyond the bounds of possibility that a schoolgirl might feel a liking for me.

And I wanted Anne to like me. I remembered with pleasure a single playful and informal gesture on her part. I had said something sardonic at her expense and she brushed my hair jokingly with her hand from behind my chair. It was done so lightly that I was barely conscious of it. I wondered whether I was justified in believing she had touched me at all. But in retrospect that action became precious. In the same way a remark she made, championing me against the teasing of my friends the Spencer-Watsons, when we were reading poetry on the lawn at Dunshay, was reassuring. As too was the mere fact of her urging us to attend a concert at the pavilion in Bournemouth where she had been recruited to swell the toll of violinists in some amateur orchestra. At that concert my eyes sought her out repeatedly in the crowd of players upon the platform, and – from the safe distance of the Grand Circle – I could feel that to me she was more important than the music.

She had become a key figure in my reactions to the school. What were all my efforts to discuss her impartially and even severely at the staff-meetings but indirect evidence of the same kind of fixation? It was a relief to tease her simply because it served as a reminder of our true relationship of schoolgirl and teacher. And yet Thursday delighted me, for on that afternoon any perfunctory facet of that relationship was laid aside and we became fellow-enthusiasts sharing the same treasure.

I know it must seem nonsense to you to hear all these excuses for a past pre-occupation. But though you may not realise it, I am defending a philosophic and, one could almost say, a moral position. That talented Frenchman André Maurois speaks impatiently of "the petty guiles of physical love", because, through our epoch's obsession with them, he thinks we "lose the incalculable forces which are generated by romantic love". The poet Robert Graves takes much the same line, maintaining that "love is a mystical emotion which civilisation has all but destroyed." Today, he says, because of what he calls "the mechanarchy in which we live", "this holy love is preserved only in young people and true poets." Here are two writers, basically realistic, who would, I believe, understand my painstaking analysis of the shadowy fringes of a fundamental emotion.

The end of term came, and I did not even take the trouble to see Anne to say good-bye to her when she left a few days before the rest of the school. Her departure passed unnoticed. This gives some idea of how little I allowed myself to indulge sentiment.

I tidied up the bungalow – we were letting it to well-liked
annual tenants – and got ready for my visit to the island. I was
going by sea. The ancient paddle-steamers, which had maintained their summer service for more than half-a-century, managed the direct journey in under two hours, which meant a great
saving of time. It was not on one of them but on the Portsmouth
ferry that our little boy had lost his native innocence and been
introduced to sea-sicknesses, remarking to his mother in surprised tones when half way across the Solent, "Mummy, the sea's
pokin' up in a lot of places!"

The sea did not "poke up" in any places for my trip, though it
might have made the voyage more interesting if it had. Any
voyage on a tripper-steamer is wearisome to people of the wrong
temperament. Even the knowledge that I was saving myself a rail
journey of two or three hours was not enough to maintain the
mood of elation in which – freed for nearly two whole months – I
set forth. The tediousness of the noisy voyage weighed heavily
upon me as I descended the gangway. And when, after a long
delay at the junction, Newport, our train steamed slowly into
the little terminus under the down, there was no figure on the
platform to meet me. Ventnor has two stations, Ventnor West
connecting with Cowes, and the other, equally small but more
important, on the east side of the little seaside town. The platform
was completely deserted, but on a bench at its side under an array
of time-tables sat a girl amazingly like Anne. For a moment I
thought that I was having hallucinations. Then I realised that it
was Anne.

"What on earth brings you here?"

"Daddy's outside in the car. We drove over because the film *As
You Like It* is on in Ventnor tonight and we thought you might like
to come to it with us. Elizabeth Bergner is Rosalind."

"Hm. I don't think I'll come. I'm tired and I've been sleeping
badly. But Reggie might. Where is he?"

"He's gone to the wrong station to meet you. He thought you
were coming on the other line. They told us at 'Sunnybrae' he'd
probably made that mistake. Daddy's offered to drive you back to
Bonchurch. Get your baggage and come."

Feeling that the age of miracles was not over, I followed her out
to the car.

"Daddy's had a great compliment. The maid at 'Sunnybrae'

went in and said, 'There's a young lady and a young gentleman outside who want to see you.' It's not the first time he's been taken for my brother."

I got into the restricted space at the back of the small sports car and we drove off. When Reggie, having discovered his mistake, returned to 'Sunnybrae', he found us there. No, he would not go with them to the film. He refused to leave a house-guest who had only that moment arrived. In any case, if he went to the film at all, he had made a half-promise to the de Vere Stackpooles to go to the second showing of *As You Like It* with them. Anne's mother was waiting at the cinema, so they must be off.

"No, we can't stay to tea, thank you. She'll be wondering already what has happened to us."

"Well, will you come to tea with us later in the week?"

"That would be very nice."

"What day? Saturday?"

"Yes. That would be all right. We know where to find you now."

At four on Saturday they arrived. Anne was wearing a grey tweed coat and skirt, the skirt rather long, as though she wished to announce to everyone that her exam was over and that she had left the schoolgirl behind. She had had her hair cut, had washed it, and it was brushed now to a silky fineness. "You look very much the young lady," I remarked, half ironically, half appreciatively, when I first saw her. Chairs were brought out and we sat on the lawn, where Reggie's white-haired, handsome father joined us. The talk turned to the writing of poetry. "Anne tells me that you haven't written a poem for two years," Anne's mother said. It was almost true, but not quite. There were just those sixteen lines which it would have been a blunder to acknowledge in present company. Her mother, a fellow poet, began to discuss the conditions most favourable to composition. We agreed that the auspicious moment for it was unpredictable. If I had been honest, I would have said, "There is certainly one favourable specific for it." And, asked to elaborate further, I could have replied enigmatically – love.

When the afternoon shadows reached our chairs, we went into the house. It had been suggested that we should play puff-billiards. Only in Bonchurch, with its Victorian associations, its memories of the young Swinburne, and its charming old ladies, such as the three survivors of the Venables family, could one come across such a game. It is played on a circular, polished mahogany board to which four, swivelled, rubber blowers are attached. The aim is to try and puff a tiny cork ball into one's opponents' well-defended cupped goal. Anne was my partner, and Reggie played with the other youthful visitor, the daughter of the headmaster of the school where Anne's father taught. There was much laughter and excitement. A really good puff would send the tiny ball round and round the circular board until it perhaps dropped into the hole guarded by the very person whose frantic blowing had been responsible for its momentum in the first instance. I looked across at Anne, waiting for the moment when she would look up, and I would be able to meet the amusement in her extraordinarily clear limpid eyes and notice the beauty of her teeth when she smiled. It was her eyes, always her eyes, those huge, half-sorrowful, half-reproachful eyes which exercised their spell over me. But now, for a few minutes, they spelt carefree happiness.

"Tea is ready," the maid announced.

We put the puff-billiards table away in its place beside the piano and went into the dining room.

It was not a long visit. They left at six. I went out with Reggie to see them off. Anne climbed into the front seat beside her father. She looked frail, gentle, flower-like; and, knowing she had two important music examinations looming, I impulsively leaned towards the open window of the car and said to her –

"Don't overwork."

Without turning her head she murmured,

"What does it matter? Who cares?"

It was said in one of those moments of sudden self-pity, frequent in the young and not unknown to most of us, even if we have been laughing heartily only a few moments before. I would have loved to have said, "I care. Surely you have suspected sometimes that I care? Your parents care. Le bon Dieu cares." But one does not say such things, least of all at the door of a small sports car as it begins to move down an avenue.

Of course I cared. Let me give you a small indication. I remember reading about this time a brochure advertising a three weeks' cruise in the Mediterranean, and thinking how wonderful it would be if I could act the role of a magician and send her away on it. What she needed was Greece. Damn music exams! It had grown chilly on the lawn before we had moved into the house and I fetched a coat from the hall for her to put round her knees. Looking at her as I had given it to her I had felt that half-defiant shyness which makes everything one says to a person an irrelevance, unreal, an attempt to cloak one's thoughts rather than to reveal them. I felt the embarrassment of those who know they are poised over a precipice. That night it delighted me when Reggie's father remarked at supper, "You are lucky if all your pupils are as charming as the one who came here today."

Reggie's leave ended a few days later, and he caught his boat at Southampton for Marseilles. I remained a little longer at Bonchurch so that I might be there when his elder brother, Walter, and his wife arrived. The place had changed hardly at all since the days of Swinburne's childhood. One paid the usual round of obligatory visits. To be shown by the pretty capped maid of the Venables sisters into their drawing-room was like a cast-back to the age of Tennyson, whom their father had known quite well. Just down the road lived de Vere Stackpoole, author of what the era acclaimed as a most daring, but actually a most innocent story, *The Blue Lagoon*. In the Stackpoole's lovely garden was a huge croquet lawn always available at any time for the use of their friends.

One afternoon we drove over to visit the poet Alfred Noyes at Orchard Bay on the far side of Ventnor. His poetry stood for all that the current trend rejected and held up to scorn. But 'The Highwayman" will continue to give pleasure. Noyes was contemplating an anthology as a riposte to the highly capricious one just published by Yeats, and I had promised to lend him certain books. When these were safely delivered, it occurred to me that we were half way to the home of Anne's parents.

"Would you ever have time to drive me on to Niton?" I said to Walter. "We're half way there already. I've a pupil there, and we said we would try and arrange tennis with them one day at the Ventnor courts."

We drove on. It was surprising what immense relief my decision immediately gave me. I had been postponing it from one day to the next in a typically indecisive manner. Now this errand to the poet Noyes had decided the matter for me.

We came into Niton – a bigger village than I expected – and stopped a man to ask him if he could direct us to "Nutkins", the cottage we were in search of. He told us the way and then added, "But you're wasting your time. I saw them go away yesterday, the whole family."

We had missed them by one day. I had dawdled and temporised, and now they were gone. But how strange of them not to have said that they were going so soon. I suggested to Walter that we should drive on in case there had been a mistake. We found the cottage, built more than a hundred years before, thatched and verandahed, rather in the style of Mrs. Gaskell's "Cranford". Going into the garden, while Walter turned the car, I looked through the bow window at the bare, sparsely-furnished room, with a number of books, a few chairs, and a rather deserted, week-end appearance. They had departed perhaps to Anne's grandfather with whom they often stayed.

I returned to Walter and climbed into the car. She was gone. Fate had answered my unvoiced request and made the decision for me. My pre-occupation with her had always been a disproportionate one. It was better not to pursue the matter any further. My psychological conflict was suddenly resolved; I now seemed able to put her out of my mind.

A few days later I sailed for Ireland to be with my wife and children. The grandeur of Donegal – the slate and azure blue of its sea, the rhythmic sweep of its deserted beaches, the brown monotony of its bogland which only unwillingly surrenders its edges to ragged fields and broken hills, all of which are washed into one another on the grey days of sloping rain – weakened for a few weeks the hold of the Dorset countryside over me.

A year or two later the war came. Arthur and Vera, their own children, and a small core of the school departed to Canada. I left Swanage and went to live in Dublin.

Twelve years passed. In the summer of 1951 I was in almost nightly attendance at the ballet, gathering material for a new book. I had abandoned teaching for a time, and though still living in Dublin, had come to stay at Wimbledon with the youngest of my three brothers-in-law. I would walk across Wimbledon Common and then take a train into London. Covent Garden is the Mecca of English ballet. The comfort of the great opera house is reassuring. Downstairs, before the performance, I used to watch strangers hurriedly consuming a plate of cold meat, salad and mayonnaise while they rested on one of the plush-covered sofas which extend round the curve of the great corridor at the back of the stalls. Upstairs the better-lit and more spacious precincts of the crush-bar offered still greater reassurance. In the interval I might allow myself the indulgence of a cup of coffee. But not always. Halfway up the wide staircase, on either side of the great mirror flanked by two pedestals surmounted on gala occasions by vases containing a wealth of flowers, were two cushioned and chintz-covered settees. Often I preferred to forego my coffee and sit there watching the audience as they flowed up from the stalls below to the crush-bar. By choosing the nearer of the two settees, one could watch the movement on both the lower and the upper flight. Frequently I sat there alone, the solitary observer of this progress. Sometimes I found myself forestalled. There was room for three persons on the settee; but I was unsociable and, when this happened, I generally elected to descend the wide staircase into the foyer and emerge into the cool of the pathway outside.

I was seated there during the second interval one evening in June, when a lady in a brown cloth dress came down the upper flight from the crush-bar towards the mirror and stopped immediately beside me, as though she had something to say to me. Almost immediately I heard her speak my name. I jumped to the conclusion that she must be a secretary with a message from the manager or from the public relations officer, an individual invariably sympathetic when it came to ringing up and asking for a press seat. I waited to hear what was wanted of me. A look of slight distress came into the eyes of the figure facing me; a look fractionally nearer humiliation than disappointment. A bystander would not have noticed it; but to me it was sufficiently arresting to make me feel I had blundered. That fleeting shadow of an expression – for it was nothing more – was enough to bring me to my senses. I rose to my feet and exclaimed in genuine delight,

"Why, you're Anne! I really do believe that you are Anne! How wonderful! How clever of you to have spotted me! And what luck you should be here tonight. I come quite often. But this is the first time I've ever encountered an ex-pupil. Tell me about yourself. You're married, aren't you? Someone said that you married at eighteen and that your husband is a schoolmaster, preferring to teach people rather than to kill them. Is that correct?"

Before she could answer, the strident warning bell to mark the end of the interval went for the second time.

"Where are you in the house? I must see you after the show."

"Down in the stalls. But I'm with a very rich relative and her lady-companion. They won't want to be kept waiting."

"All right. I'll hurry down. If you watch the stairs I'll come quickly. In any case we can't miss each other in the foyer."

Nor did we. I caught sight of her immediately on the far side of the lounge with two middle-aged women pre-occupied with their furs. To my indignation I heard one of them say to her, as I neared them, "Very well. You can walk with him as far as the car." She might have been giving permission to a housemaid to accompany the third under-footman as far as the pillar-box. Anne did not introduce me; nor did they show any inclination to be introduced. The limit of concession seemed to have been reached in those words "as far as the car". I am a touchy individual. If no-one save a duke takes precedence at table over a member of the French Academy, it is my secret opinion that a poet should rank above the possessor of any Rolls Royce or Daimler on the road.

It was a Daimler, parked alongside the pathway less than a hundred yards down the road in the direction of the Strand. We had practically no time for conversation as we made our way there. And as soon as we reached the car, followed closely by its owner and her friend, I said abruptly, "Well, good-night, Anne. Lovely to see you!" turned on my heel, and walked quickly away. My voice must have reached them clearly, and I hoped I had made it sufficiently plain that I had not any inclination to outstay my welcome. Crossing Waterloo Bridge I thought how strange it was not to have recognised her. All recognitions are perhaps instigated by association. But that night I had started from an entirely wrong association, or rather a wrong premise. I would have said that she was unforgettable, and in the far-reaching perspective of life she was, of course, unforgettable. But, though she had not changed so greatly, I had seen her as a stranger. Running up the great stone steps of the station I just caught a train to Wimbledon, not that there was ever any trouble in doing so, there are always plenty. As I walked across the south side of the common, with its soft riding-track under my feet, the significance of my chance encounter began to lose its force. It became a mere coincidence to be mentioned casually to my brother-in-law at his hurried breakfast next morning, "A funny thing happened last night . . ."

I know quite well what my relation of this incident will have said to you: "Everything is ephemeral. Even love". We men are ephemera. We float upon the current of time as tiny pieces of wood float upon the current of a river. Sometimes two of these fragments are drawn into an eddy, to whirl madly round or to revolve slowly. They may become aligned, float parallel to one another and even touch, and for a while may seem to have escaped from that ceaseless movement which is bearing everything away on its surface. In their backwater they appear to be safe and stationary; but they are bound, sooner or later, to be drawn back into the current and to be carried forward again towards the relentless and ever-greedy sea. It is only a question of time before that momentary halt which love makes in our lives is brought to a conclusion. Still more is this true if the occasion is one when we are not even sure that we did love in any real sense, but were merely drawn briefly into the orbit of another personality. Surely if I had loved I would have swallowed my pride and stayed for a minute or two longer by the side of the well-polished Daimler? On reflection, I am not so sure. In an unexpected context, one can make mistakes.

Two years after our encounter at Covent Garden, I went down to stay for three or four days with Arthur and Vera Hickson. They were back from their years of exile in Canada where they had brought their family and a small group of other children when the school suspended operations early in the war. The Old Lady was dead, and Arthur had moved down to Cauldron Barn and turned farmer in preference to re-starting the school. He would presently own a farm of considerable size, enlarged by a number of wise purchases along Knitson Lane, which had been declared a part of Swanage's "green belt". There, under the downs, ample room had been found for pigs and sheep as well as for a very fine herd of Jersey cows. I found him and Vera unchanged. They were as friendly as ever, and as devoted to their numerous pets and livestock. But, alas, when I entered the four stalls in the stable, I found not Sally and Betty but a mountain of books removed from the school when the soldiers had taken over during the war. Those dusty somewhat battered volumes, in great heaps, were like a reproachful nudge from the past. I had survived all other reminders of the 'thirties with fortitude, but this one distressed me.

On the third morning of my visit, Arthur announced that he

had to drive over to Blandford on some business with Bryanston School. I knew that Anne's husband had taught there and was now teaching in the sister-school for girls not far away. My host confirmed that Anne still lived in the Bryanston grounds.

"If I ring her up and make sure that she will be there, would you take me with you?"

"Certainly. But you'll have to ask her to give you lunch. We shall be lunching with the Bryanston headmaster."

It was simpler than I anticipated. Anne answered the phone. Yes I could come and take pot luck. Her husband unfortunately would be away teaching and would not be home until the evening.

"You know that I run a small nursery school here for children of the Bryanston staff? But they'll have finished by the time you come and will have gone home. Yes, it will be very nice to see you."

June may be the perfect Dorset month, but September runs it close. It was September now. We started off by Knitson Lane because Arthur wished to look at a herd of young heifers which were grazing there. When we emerged from under the down at Corfe I looked up at the narrow, perpendicular ruin of Corfe Castle on its cone-shaped mound and thought of those July evenings when we would go to Corfe and sit on the grass on the steep slope below the castle to listen to the Balliol Players in one of their informal yearly productions of a play by Aristophanes. All performances on this vacation tour were out of doors; the setting was ideal and the cast seemed to derive quite as much amusement from their efforts as their audience did. The light slowly dimmed; the summer evening seemed reluctant to yield to darkness, and when we rose from our rugs the long outline of Nine Barrow Down was at once gentle and formidable against what remained of the saffron-streaked sky above Studland. It was a regular event, a breathing space in our active days, linking the Athens of Pericles with the Dorset of Hardy. And now, as Arthur drove on towards Wareham there were further memories; of cycle rides to Arne; and of the Canadian canoe, used at Oxford by my wife when she was at St. Hugh's, and by her three brothers at Christchurch, and bequeathed to us just before the war, then taken to Wareham and left to languish there for the war-years in the rafters of old Habgood's boat shed; in fact for so long that we never had the face to reclaim it.

All this and, equally, the great stretch of moorland which lay between Wareham and Bere Regis, unspoilt even by the mock-battles of tanks, put me in a nostalgic mood long before we reached Blandford, and drove out of that clean, self-assured, 16th century town to Bryanston Park, only a mile away. There I enquired my way to Anne's abode, a small, neat, almost "Jane Austen residence" amongst the trees at the foot of the hill behind the great red-brick building with its Portland stone dressings. I promised Arthur and Vera faithfully that I would be back beside the car at five o'clock and we separated each to his own business.

I remember little of the visit. The situation seemed an ideal one for a nursery-school of nine or ten children, but I could hardly believe that my paragon on horseback should be so acceptant of life's limitations as to be running an establishment of this nature. I saw no children. They had already gone home, and I quickly put them from my mind, as though they were an interference to memory, something to be banished because they did not fit into the picture. And yet Anne said enough to show that she was no time-server taking her responsibilities – all hers, she had no assistant – unnecessarily seriously, neither gushing nor grumbling where her small pupils were concerned. Actually she would presently migrate to the world of art and creativity, helping to make Blandford a centre of theatrical activity and winning quite a reputation for herself as a producer and as an actress in the plays of Ibsen, Tchekov, and others.

After lunch we went into the sitting-room and sat side by side on the sofa, talking about the past. I felt that it was at once, for me, a romantic occasion; and, at the same time, one strangely lacking in romance. Like Yeats, I could boast of the phoenix known to me in youth; and now the phoenix had come to rest here. What had I expected for her? I was not quite sure. I had never actually pictured her exercising an hypnotic effect upon a Queen's Hall audience with her violin; or starting a new movement in poetry; or going on the stage and making Tess of the d'Urbervilles as heartrending as she had once made Richard the Second for us in the big dining-hall. All these had been possibilities. And yet, to tell the truth, I had never troubled myself with anticipation for her at all. I had only wished her happiness. Happiness and love, for she seemed equally made for both.

She gave me tea in good time, for Arthur and Vera must not be kept waiting. Then we got into her car. She had offered to drive me to the foot of the hill, leaving me only the effort of climbing the path through the trees to the drive where their car was waiting. It was a matter of less than a mile, and we sat together talking in the car for a few minutes after arrival, for there was no need to hurry. Then I put out my hand, rested it for a moment on her knee beside me, and said, "Well, good-bye Anne, and God bless you."

She leaned over and kissed me on the mouth. It was entirely unexpected, a magical moment for anyone as shy as myself. Her kiss was the warm spontaneous kiss of genuine affection, something which silenced words rather than prompted them. Another man might have seen it as a god-sent opportunity for further exchanges, the throwing open of a closed door, the chance to satisfy a long hunger. But not in my case. She probably knew her man. It was a safe kiss to give, a kiss simply of remembrance with a slight tincture perhaps of gratitude.

I got out of the car as though nothing extraordinary had happened. There was not the smallest sign to indicate, even faintly, my inner reaction to the event. I could not have been more insouciant if it had been a wave of the hand. Whereas actually I was overwhelmed. The Hicksons were just coming out of the school when I reached the drive. We drove home in almost complete silence on my part. I have no doubt that they realised that my visit had meant a great deal to me. Silence was therefore excusable in the circumstances. The much-discussed "intermittences" of the heart are of course a fact. You will have said, "But he met her at Covent Garden and didn't even know whom she was. And now, after two minutes side by side in a car and because of a momentary impulse of generous affection on her part, he is overwhelmed. That doesn't say much for either the depth or longevity of his devotion."

I am not here to defend or to explain my own vagaries of mood. All I would point out is that one of the recognisable facets of love is that it places us outside time. On our way to the Daimler, I was emphatically anchored in time; time-enslaved. I felt, if not outraged, then at least tetchily annoyed by the hauteur of her unpleasant hostess. If anything was calculated to limit my consciousness to the immediate present, this feeling of angry resentment was. Whereas what had just happened to me on my way up to Bryanston was destined to have precisely the reverse effect. It set me outside time and reopened my eyes to the former activities of my heart. One enters a darkened room, gropes to one side of the door and switches on the light. And instantly the whole room is made luminous, in this case by the incandescent glow of the past. That was exactly what had occurred. I was once more attuned to something which had taken place long before. Anne's action had released a flood of memories which had never really been entirely submerged. She had re-created for me vividly all that I had once felt so that the mood of the present, freed from all temporal limitations, had suddenly become the mood of the past.

I sat in a state of bemused happiness for almost the whole of the drive. How right Kingsley Amis was when he wrote – although in an entirely different context:-

Sex is a momentary itch,
Love never lets you go.

As we drove towards Swanage, I kept thinking, "So she did like you a little. She must have done so to have kissed you on the lips as she did." And then the sense of irony would over-take me and I would think, "Funny to have waited seventeen years for a kiss. Well, it was worth waiting for!"

When a player strikes a note, or plucks the strings of an instrument, the note sounds and then begins gradually to die away. But the faint ghost of it persists. It remains, almost inaudible, until the foot is lifted finally from the pedal, or till the hand is placed firmly flat upon the harp-strings. Only then does the chord cease to vibrate. It is just the same with the music which life makes for us. It has a resonance all its own.

NOTE

The Pupil is a corollary to my other autobiographical works and is based, like them, upon lengthy entries in my journal, made at the time, or shortly afterwards. The years passed and when I began to write the narrative, I put it – although it was an entirely truthful confession – into the mouth of a fictional character who related the events to a friend. I have to thank Peter Kuch for his most generous help in changing this structure and eliminating any superfluous audience. Also for his sensitive discernment of various essential inflexions. My debt to the indefatigable Rita Lorigan is quite as great. Uncomplainingly, she decoded passages of manuscript which I myself was unable to interpret and retyped a succession of versions each in turn destined to be rejected.

SOME VIEWS OF MONK GIBBON'S OTHER WORK

"The self-confessed aim of Monk Gibbon is 'to turn life into the word' . . . He himself is endowed with a poetic sensibility which has sharpened his awareness of the tiniest physical sensations, revealing them in all their loveliness, sometimes just for their own sake and sometimes for a wider set of associations which they suggest."

Barbara Wright, F.T.C.D., in *The Dublin Magazine*.

"What gives this tale its substance is its author's scrupulous concern with emotional shades; his book is almost an essay on the things which produce the feeling of love . . . the enjoyment of life, the fortune of unexpected meetings, the attitude of those about one to what he does, it is in the marginal emotions, the feelings that run along the fringe of loving that he is most apt."

Punch on *The Climate of Love*.

"The poems are remarkable in their simplicity of form and in their elaboration of thought. I find myself picking up this volume when I had meant to leave it lying, which is the test of really good poetry."

Rebecca West

"You have found your voice and the words and emotion will deepen with life and study and if both bring you to some tragic situation you will have all the poet needs."

W.B. Yeats

"His descriptions of the ordinary routine and of special assignments – in recognisable hazard of life – are masterly; an immense amount of pertinent detail, accurately and engagingly described. . . Few could diifer more from Monk Gibbon on the particular moral issue than this reviewer; but few could more admire the honesty and sincerity of the record, the grace and dignity of the prose."

Lord Reith of *Inglorious Soldier* in The Spectator

"There are not many writers who are willing to let their experience settle and refine, so that what we get is gold."

Richard Church, on *Mount Ida* in *The Spectator*.

"If there is a better prose stylist in this country – again in the 19th century sense of essay and argument – I do not know of their work . . . Monk Gibbon's prose with its fresh, accurate and unsentimental view of disparate events recreates an altogether more complex world: seal-hunting, the ballet, torn loyalties – things loved for their own sake and recorded as they were. It is a considerable achievement. And in this, as in much else, Monk Gibbon has remained himself."

Eavan Boland in *The Irish Times*.

"You have found yourself. I read *The Seals* with interest from sentence to sentence of your admirable prose, interest nowhere flagging, because your own intentness of eye and mind nowhere lapsed. How good it is in a book to come upon this consuming interest in what the eye casually rests on, bird on rock or coloured sea or sky, as if there was beneath consciousness the knowledge that these were all part of ourselves. . . . I like the wisdom you drop so effortlessly as if it was natural to be wise. . . . I felt when reading your island adventure that it was as good to read you as to go out to the island itself. . . . I hope you will write more in this mood. *I am tempted to desire for you that your life should be all holiday and a busy idleness, like those hours on the island. You are far better reading than a novel*, and I congratulate you on coming to yourself so early. Many of us never come to ourselves at all.

Yours sincerely,
AE."

Letter from 'A.E.' (George Russell) to the author